The Minister's Black Veil

A Dark Parable of Secrets, Judgment & the Fear Behind the Mask of Morality

A Modern Translation
Adapted for the Contemporary Reader

Nathaniel Hawthorne

Translated by Tim Zengerink

Table of Contents

Preface
Message To The Reader

Rebuilding the Greatest Library in Human History

Thousands of years ago, the Library of Alexandria was the heart of global knowledge — a sanctuary where the wisdom of every known civilization was gathered and shared freely.

And then, it was lost.

Now, we're rebuilding it — and you are invited to join us.

At the Library of Alexandria, we've set out to make every book available to every person on Earth — not just in print, but in every language, every format, and for every reader.

Here's how we do it:

- **Deluxe Print Editions at True Printing Cost** - Order any book as a high-quality paperback, elegant hardcover, or stunning boxset — and only pay what it costs to print. No markups. No middlemen.
- **Unlimited Access to the Greatest Works** - Enjoy thousands of timeless classics — from Plato to Shakespeare to Tolstoy — in beautiful, modern eBook and audiobook editions. Read and listen without limits — for every reader, everywhere.
- **Modern Translations for Every Language & Dialect** - We're reimagining the classics in clear, accessible language — and translating them into every dialect imaginable. Everyone deserves to understand humanity's greatest ideas.

When you visit **LibraryofAlexandria.com**, you're not just accessing books — you're joining a global movement to restore, preserve, and share the wisdom of civilization.

Join us today at LibraryofAlexandria.com

Together, we'll ensure the light of human wisdom never fades again.

With gratitude,

The Modern Library of Alexandria Team

Visit:
www.libraryofalexandria.com
Or scan the code below:

Introduction

Hawthorne's Exploration of Sin, Guilt, and Social Judgment

Nathaniel Hawthorne's *The Minister's Black Veil*, first published in 1836 in *The Token and Atlantic Souvenir*, stands as one of the most enigmatic and allegorically rich short stories in American literature. Known for his preoccupation with themes of hidden sin, moral hypocrisy, and the dark undercurrents of Puritan society, Hawthorne uses this tale to probe the human psyche and challenge the superficial piety that masks deeper truths. It is not merely a story about a minister who dons a black veil; it is a parable about the universal human condition—our fear of being truly known, our collective guilt, and the judgment we cast upon those who dare to confront uncomfortable truths.

The story centers around Reverend Mr. Hooper, a minister in a small Puritan town, who one day appears before his congregation wearing a black veil that obscures his face. This simple yet startling act throws the entire community into a state of unease. The veil becomes a source of gossip, fear, and speculation. What sin, they wonder, is the minister hiding? What dark secret lies behind this unsettling symbol? As the narrative unfolds, the veil transforms from a mere piece of cloth into a powerful emblem of the hidden sins and private guilts that every person carries within themselves.

One of the most striking aspects of *The Minister's Black Veil* is Hawthorne's ability to create an atmosphere of profound moral tension without relying on supernatural elements or violent events. There are no ghostly apparitions or dramatic confessions—only a quiet, pervasive sense of unease that grows as the veil becomes a permanent part of Mr. Hooper's identity. Through this seemingly simple symbol, Hawthorne examines the complexities of human nature, the fear of vulnerability, and the ways in which society reacts to those who break its unspoken rules.

The black veil is not merely a personal gesture; it is a challenge to the community's collective conscience. By wearing it, Mr. Hooper forces those around him to confront their own hidden transgressions, their unacknowledged sins, and their fear of being judged. The story suggests that the horror people feel at the sight of the veil is not because of what it reveals about Mr. Hooper, but because of what it reflects back onto them. It is a mirror in which they see their own hypocrisy and moral frailty.

Hawthorne's background and literary style play a significant role in shaping the themes of this story. As a descendant of Puritan ancestors, some of whom were involved in the Salem witch trials, Hawthorne felt a personal connection to the rigid moral codes and dark history of early New England. His writing often grapples with the lingering effects of Puritanism on the American psyche, particularly the tension between public piety and private guilt. In *The Minister's Black Veil,* this tension is palpable, as the community outwardly values morality and virtue but is inwardly disturbed by the suggestion that everyone harbors hidden sins.

The Symbolism of the Veil and the Fear of Truth

The black veil in Hawthorne's story is one of the most potent and enduring symbols in American literature. Its meaning is deliberately ambiguous, which allows for a wide range of interpretations. Some readers view it as a symbol of secret sin—a physical manifestation of the spiritual darkness that Mr. Hooper, and indeed all people, carry within themselves. Others see it as a commentary on the human tendency to hide behind social masks, concealing our true thoughts and emotions for fear of judgment or rejection.

What makes the veil so unsettling is not just its appearance but the way it transforms relationships. The townspeople, who once respected and admired Mr. Hooper, now find themselves recoiling from him. His sermons, once inspiring, become chilling, as though the veil gives his words a new, more disturbing weight. Even his fiancée, Elizabeth, pleads with him to remove the veil, suggesting that its presence creates an insurmountable barrier between them. Yet Mr. Hooper refuses, insisting that the veil must remain as a constant reminder of the truths people would rather ignore.

This refusal is crucial to understanding the story's deeper meaning. Mr. Hooper is not wearing the veil because of a specific sin or crime; rather, he wears it to symbolize the universal nature of sin and the isolation it creates. By embracing the symbol of guilt and shame, he becomes both a spiritual leader and a pariah—a man who is feared, misunderstood, and ultimately alienated from those he seeks to teach.

The veil also raises questions about the nature of truth and the fear it inspires. People prefer comforting illusions to harsh realities, and the veil, by exposing the hidden aspects of the human soul, disrupts this preference. In this sense, the story is as much about the townspeople as it is about Mr. Hooper. Their discomfort with the veil reflects their unwillingness to confront their own imperfections. Hawthorne suggests that true self-knowledge is both necessary and terrifying—that to look honestly at one's soul is to see not only goodness but also darkness.

Moreover, the veil serves as a metaphor for the barriers that exist between all human beings. We are all, in a sense, hidden behind our own veils—masks of politeness, social roles, and unspoken fears. Mr. Hooper's literal veil makes visible what is normally invisible: the distance and separation that come from our unwillingness to reveal our true selves. In this way, the story is not just a critique of Puritanism but a timeless reflection on the human condition.

Hawthorne's Craft, Legacy, and the Reader's Journey

Hawthorne's literary style is characterized by rich symbolism, moral ambiguity, and a deep engagement with the psychological and spiritual dimensions of life. In *The Minister's Black Veil*, these qualities are on full display. The narrative is concise yet layered with meaning, every detail contributing to the story's haunting atmosphere. Hawthorne does not explain the veil or resolve its mystery; instead, he invites readers to grapple with its significance, to question their own assumptions about sin, morality, and human nature.

The story's structure is deceptively simple. It begins with the minister's appearance in the veil, follows the community's reaction, and ends with Mr. Hooper's deathbed scene, where he declares that everyone wears a black veil. This final statement is both a revelation and a condemnation, suggesting that the townspeople's judgment of Mr. Hooper is hypocritical because they, too, hide behind masks of their own making. The ending reinforces the story's central message: that the fear of being truly known—of having one's inner self exposed—is a universal human experience.

Hawthorne's exploration of these themes resonates across time and cultures. The black veil has become a powerful metaphor in literary criticism, psychology, and even popular culture. It represents not only hidden sin but also the broader concept of the unknown—the aspects of ourselves and others that remain concealed. In an era of social media and curated identities, the story's insights into the masks we wear and the judgments we cast feel more relevant than ever.

For readers, *The Minister's Black Veil* offers both a challenge and an invitation. It challenges us to confront the ways in which we hide our true selves and judge others for doing the same. At the same time, it invites us to reflect on the nature of forgiveness, compassion, and understanding. Mr. Hooper's life, marked by isolation and misunderstanding, raises difficult questions: Is it better to reveal the truth, even if it leads to rejection? Or is it more humane to maintain the comforting illusions that allow society to function?

As you approach this story, consider the layers of meaning embedded in Hawthorne's prose. Pay attention to the way he uses imagery—the contrast between light and darkness, the solemnity of the church setting, the unsettling presence of the veil—to create a mood of quiet but unrelenting tension. Reflect on the reactions of the townspeople and what they reveal about human nature. And, most importantly, consider the veil you might wear in your own life, the secrets and fears that remain hidden, and how they shape your relationships with others.

In conclusion, *The Minister's Black Veil* is not simply a story about a minister or a piece of cloth; it is a profound meditation on the human soul, the masks we wear, and the truths we fear. Hawthorne's ability to weave moral complexity, psychological insight, and symbolic power into a brief narrative is a testament to his mastery as a writer. As you read this story, let it unsettle you, provoke you, and inspire you to look beyond the surface—to see the veils that surround you, and perhaps, the ones you wear yourself.

The Minister's Black Veil

A Parable

The church caretaker stood in the entrance of Milford's meetinghouse, pulling vigorously on the bell rope. The elderly villagers came walking slowly down the street. Children with cheerful faces skipped happily alongside their parents or copied a more serious walk, proudly aware of their Sunday best. Well-dressed single men glanced sideways at the attractive young women, imagining that the Sunday sunlight made them even more beautiful than during the week. When most of the crowd had flowed into the entrance, the caretaker began to ring the bell slowly, keeping his gaze fixed on Reverend Mr. Hooper's door. The first sight of the minister's figure was the cue for the bell to stop its calling.

"But what has good Parson Hooper got upon his face?" cried the sexton, in astonishment.

Everyone within earshot immediately turned around and saw what appeared to be Mr. Hooper walking slowly in his thoughtful manner toward the meeting-house. They all reacted with surprise at the same time, showing more amazement than if some unfamiliar minister had arrived to clean the cushions of Mr. Hooper's pulpit.

"Are you certain it's our minister?" Goodman Gray asked the sexton.

"It's definitely good Mr. Hooper," the sexton replied. "He was supposed to switch pulpits with Pastor Shute from Westbury, but Pastor Shute sent word yesterday to excuse himself because he has to preach a funeral sermon."

The reason for all this astonishment might seem quite trivial. Mr. Hooper, a refined gentleman of approximately thirty years old who remained unmarried, was dressed with proper clerical tidiness, as though a devoted wife had starched his collar and removed the week's dust from his Sunday clothing. Only one aspect of his appearance stood out as unusual. Wrapped around his forehead and draped down across his face, hanging so low that his breathing caused it to flutter, Mr. Hooper wore a black veil. Upon closer examination, it appeared to be made of two layers of crepe fabric, which completely hid his facial features except for his mouth and chin, though it likely didn't obstruct his vision beyond casting a darker tone over everything he saw, both living and lifeless. With this somber covering before him, the good Mr. Hooper continued forward with slow and measured steps, slightly hunched and gazing downward, as thoughtful men often do, while still offering friendly nods to those parishioners who remained waiting on the church steps. However, they were so stunned by his appearance that they barely acknowledged his greeting in return.

"I can't really feel like good Mr. Hooper's face is behind that piece of black cloth," said the sexton.

"I don't like it," grumbled an elderly woman as she shuffled into the meeting-house. "He has transformed himself into something terrible simply by concealing his face."

"Our minister has lost his mind!" shouted Goodman Gray, chasing after him through the doorway.

Word had spread about some mysterious occurrence involving Mr. Hooper before he arrived at the meeting-house, and it had stirred up the entire congregation. Few people could stop themselves from craning their necks toward the door; many stood up and turned around completely; while several young boys climbed onto the benches and jumped down again, making a tremendous noise. There was widespread commotion, with women's dresses rustling and men's feet shuffling, completely contrary to the quiet stillness that should accompany a minister's entrance. But Mr. Hooper seemed not to notice his congregation's agitation. He walked in with barely audible footsteps, nodded his head gently to the pews on both sides, and bowed as he passed his eldest parishioner, a white-haired great-grandfather who sat in an armchair in the center of the aisle. It was peculiar to watch how gradually this respected elder became aware of something unusual about his pastor's appearance. He didn't seem to fully share in the widespread amazement until Mr. Hooper had climbed the steps and presented himself in the pulpit, facing his congregation with only the black veil as an exception. That enigmatic symbol was never removed even once. It trembled with his steady breathing as he announced the psalm, it cast its darkness between him and the sacred text as he read the Scriptures, and while he prayed, the veil rested heavily on his raised face. Was he trying to conceal it from the fearsome Being he was addressing?

The impact of this simple piece of black cloth was so powerful that several sensitive women had to leave the church. However, the minister may have found the sight of his pale-faced congregation just as frightening as they found his black veil.

Mr. Hooper was known as a good preacher, though not a particularly dynamic one: he worked to guide his congregation toward heaven through gentle, convincing methods rather than driving them there with forceful biblical proclamations. The sermon he delivered that day showed the same style and approach as his usual preaching, but something—whether in the message itself or in the listeners' minds—made it the most powerful sermon they had ever heard from their pastor. It carried a darker tone than usual, reflecting Mr. Hooper's naturally somber disposition. His topic focused on hidden sins and those painful secrets we keep from our closest loved ones, and would gladly hide even from ourselves, forgetting that God sees everything. His words carried an mysterious power. Every person in the congregation, from the most innocent young woman to the most hardened man, felt as though the preacher had somehow seen past his frightening veil and uncovered their secret wrongdoings in action or thought. Many pressed their folded hands against their chests. There was nothing frightening in Mr. Hooper's actual words—no harshness at all—yet with each quiver of his sad voice, the listeners trembled. An unexpected sadness accompanied their fear. The congregation was so aware that something unusual had changed in their minister that they wished for a gust of wind to blow away the veil, almost convinced they would see a stranger's face beneath it, even though the body, movements, and voice were unmistakably Mr. Hooper's.

When the church service ended, people rushed out in improper disorder, anxious to share their suppressed astonishment, and feeling their spirits lift the moment the black veil disappeared from view. Some formed small groups, clustering tightly together with everyone whispering toward the center; others walked home by themselves, lost in quiet thought; still others spoke loudly and violated the sanctity of the Sabbath with showy laughter. A few nodded their wise heads, suggesting they could solve the mystery, while one or two declared there was no mystery whatsoever, only that Mr. Hooper's eyes had been weakened by late-night reading and needed protection from the light.

After a short pause, good Mr. Hooper emerged, walking behind his congregation. He turned his covered face from one group to another, showing proper respect to the elderly, greeting the middle-aged with warm dignity as their friend and spiritual leader, welcoming the young people with both authority and affection, and placing his hands on the children's heads to bless them. This had always been his practice on the Sabbath. The people responded to his kindness with strange and confused expressions. No one, unlike previous times, sought the privilege of walking beside their pastor. Old Squire Saunders—surely through an unintentional oversight—failed to invite Mr. Hooper to his dinner table, where the good minister had traditionally blessed the meal nearly every Sunday since arriving at the parish. He therefore returned to the parsonage, and just as he was about to close the door, he was seen looking back at the people, all of whom kept their eyes focused on the minister. A melancholy smile appeared faintly beneath the black veil and wavered around his lips, shimmering as he vanished from sight.

"How odd," said a woman, "that an ordinary black veil, like any woman might wear on her hat, should become such a frightening thing on Mr. Hooper's face!"

"There must be something wrong with Mr. Hooper's mind," remarked her husband, the town doctor. "But the most peculiar thing about this whole situation is how this odd behavior affects even a level-headed person like me. That black veil, even though it only covers our minister's face, casts its shadow over his entire being and makes him appear ghostly from head to toe. Don't you feel the same way?"

"I absolutely do," the lady replied; "and I wouldn't want to be alone with him for anything in the world. I'm surprised he isn't afraid to be alone with himself."

"Men sometimes are so," said her husband.

The afternoon service took place under similar circumstances. When it ended, the bell rang out for the funeral of a young woman. Her family and friends had gathered inside the house while more distant acquaintances stood around the doorway, discussing the good qualities of the deceased, when their conversation was interrupted by the arrival of Mr. Hooper, still wearing his black veil. Now it seemed like a fitting symbol. The minister entered the room where the body lay and leaned over the coffin to say a final goodbye to his departed parishioner. As he bent down, the veil hung straight down from his forehead, so that if her eyelids had not been closed forever, the dead young woman might have glimpsed his face. Could Mr. Hooper have been afraid of her gaze, causing him to pull back the black veil so quickly? Someone who observed this encounter between the dead and the living didn't hesitate to claim that at the exact moment when the clergyman's face was revealed, the corpse had trembled slightly, causing the burial shroud and linen cap to rustle, even though her expression maintained the stillness of death. A superstitious elderly woman was the only person to witness this strange event.

From the coffin, Mr. Hooper moved into the mourners' chamber, and then to the top of the staircase to deliver the funeral prayer. The prayer was gentle and deeply moving, filled with grief, yet so infused with heavenly hope that it seemed as though the faint music of an angelic harp, played by the deceased's fingers, could be heard beneath the minister's most sorrowful words. The congregation shuddered, though they only vaguely grasped his meaning, when he prayed that they, himself, and all humanity might be prepared, as he believed this young woman had been, for that terrible moment when the veil would be torn from their faces. The pallbearers slowly carried the coffin outside, followed by the mourners, casting gloom over the entire street, with the dead leading the procession and Mr. Hooper in his black veil bringing up the rear.

"Why are you looking back?" one person in the procession asked their companion.

"I had a feeling," she replied, "that the minister and the maiden's spirit were walking hand in hand."

"And I felt the same way at that exact moment," said the other.

That night the most beautiful couple in Milford village was going to get married. Even though people considered Mr. Hooper a sad man, he had a calm happiness for events like this that often brought out understanding smiles where more lively joy would have been wasted. No other part of his personality made him more loved than this quality. The wedding guests waited for him to arrive with growing restlessness, hoping that the strange fear that had surrounded him all day would finally go away. But that's not what happened. When Mr. Hooper arrived, the first thing everyone noticed was that same terrible black veil that had made the funeral even more gloomy and could only mean something bad for the wedding. The effect on the guests was so immediate that it seemed like a dark cloud had rolled out from under the black fabric and made the candlelight dimmer. The bride and groom stood before the minister, but the bride's cold fingers shook in the trembling hand of the groom, and her deathly pale skin made people whisper that the young woman who had been buried just hours earlier had come back from her grave to get married. If there was ever another wedding so depressing, it was that famous one where they rang the wedding bell like a funeral bell.

After completing the ceremony, Mr. Hooper lifted a glass of wine to his lips, offering good wishes to the newly married couple with gentle humor that should have lit up the guests' faces like warm light from a fireplace. At that moment, catching sight of his reflection in the mirror, the black veil filled his own soul with the same terror it brought to everyone else. His body trembled, his lips turned pale, he spilled the untouched wine onto the carpet and ran out into the night, for the Earth too wore her black veil.

The next day, the entire village of Milford could talk about nothing but Parson Hooper's black veil. The veil itself, along with the mystery it concealed, became the main topic of conversation for neighbors who met on the street and for women chatting at their open windows. It was the first piece of news the tavern owner shared with his customers. Children chattered about it as they walked to school. One mischievous child covered his face with an old black handkerchief, which frightened his friends so badly that he became scared himself and nearly lost his composure from his own prank.

It was striking that among all the meddlesome and intrusive people in the parish, not a single person dared to ask Mr. Hooper directly why he was doing this. Up until now, whenever there seemed to be even the slightest need for such intervention, he had never been short of advisors and had never shown any reluctance to follow their guidance. If he made any mistakes at all, it was due to such an agonizing level of self-doubt that even the gentlest criticism would make him view a harmless action as a sin. Yet, despite being so familiar with this endearing flaw, none

15

of his parishioners chose to make the black veil a topic of friendly discussion. There was a sense of fear, neither openly admitted nor carefully hidden, that made each person pass the responsibility to someone else, until finally it seemed necessary to send a group of church representatives to address Mr. Hooper about the mystery before it could become a scandal. Never had a delegation performed its duties so poorly. The minister welcomed them with warm politeness, but fell silent after they sat down, leaving his visitors with the entire burden of bringing up their important matter. The subject, one might assume, was clear enough. There was the black veil wrapped around Mr. Hooper's forehead, hiding every feature above his calm mouth, on which they could occasionally see the hint of a sad smile. But that piece of fabric, in their minds, seemed to hang down in front of his heart, representing a terrible secret between him and them. If only the veil were removed, they might discuss it openly, but not until then. So they sat for a long time, silent, bewildered, and shifting uncomfortably under Mr. Hooper's gaze, which they sensed was focused on them with an unseen intensity. Eventually, the representatives returned embarrassed to those who had sent them, declaring the matter too serious to be handled except by a council of churches, or perhaps even requiring a General Synod.

But there was one person in the village who wasn't frightened by the fear that the black veil had created in everyone else. When the church officials came back without any explanation, or even daring to ask for one, she decided with the quiet strength that defined her character to clear away the strange darkness that seemed to be gathering around Mr. Hooper, growing deeper with each passing moment. As his engaged wife, it was her right to know what the black veil was hiding. During the minister's first visit after this incident, she brought up the topic with straightforward honesty that made the conversation easier for both of them. After he had taken his seat, she stared intently at the veil, but she couldn't see any of the terrible darkness that had so intimidated the crowd; it was simply two layers of black fabric hanging from his forehead down to his mouth, moving gently with each breath he took.

"No," she said out loud, smiling, "there's nothing frightening about this piece of black cloth, except that it covers a face I'm always happy to see. Come on, good sir; let the sunshine come out from behind the cloud. First take off your black veil, then tell me why you put it on."

Mr. Hooper's smile flickered weakly.

"There will come a time," he said, "when all of us will remove our masks. Please don't take offense, dear friend, if I continue to wear this black veil until that moment arrives."

"Your words are also puzzling," the young woman replied. "Please explain what you mean more clearly."

"Elizabeth, I will," he said, "as much as my promise allows me to. Understand, then, that this veil represents something symbolic, and I am obligated to wear it always, whether in brightness or shadow, when alone or in front of crowds, and just as I do with strangers, so I must with my close friends. No human eye will ever see it removed. This gloomy covering must keep me apart from the world; even you, Elizabeth, can never get past it."

"What terrible suffering has happened to you," she asked earnestly, "that you would close your eyes to hope forever?"

"If it's a sign of mourning," Mr. Hooper replied, "then I, like most other people, probably have sorrows dark enough to be represented by a black veil."

"But what if people refuse to believe that it represents innocent grief?" Elizabeth pressed. "Even though you are loved and respected, there might be rumors that you're hiding your face because you're aware of some secret sin. For the sake of your sacred position, you must put an end to this scandal."

The color rose into her cheeks as she hinted at the nature of the rumors that were already spreading throughout the village. But Mr. Hooper's gentleness did not abandon him. He even smiled again—that same sorrowful smile which always seemed like a dim glimmer of light emerging from the darkness beneath the veil.

"If I hide my face because of sorrow, there's reason enough for it," he simply answered; "and if I cover it because of secret sin, what person wouldn't do the same?" And with this mild but unshakeable stubbornness, he resisted all her pleas.

Elizabeth remained silent for a long time. For several moments she seemed lost in thought, likely considering what new approaches she might use to pull her lover away from such a dark obsession, which, if it meant anything at all, might be a sign of mental illness. Despite having a stronger character than his, tears streamed down her face. But suddenly, as if in an instant, a new emotion replaced her sadness: her gaze became unconsciously fixed on the black veil, and like a sudden darkness falling through the air, its terrors surrounded her. She stood up and trembled before him.

"And do you feel it now, finally?" he said sadly.

She didn't respond, but covered her eyes with her hand and turned to leave the room. He rushed forward and grabbed her arm.

"Be patient with me, Elizabeth!" he cried out with intense emotion. "Don't abandon me even though this veil must remain between us here on earth. Be mine, and in the afterlife there will be no veil covering my face, no darkness separating our souls. It's only a mortal veil; it won't last for eternity. Oh, you have no idea how lonely I am, and how terrified I feel being alone behind my black veil! Don't leave me trapped in this wretched darkness forever."

"Pull back the veil just once and look at my face," she said.

"Never! It cannot be!" replied Mr. Hooper.

"Then farewell!" said Elizabeth.

She pulled her arm away from his hold and walked slowly toward the exit, stopping at the doorway to cast one final, trembling look that appeared to almost pierce through the enigma of the dark veil. Yet even in his sorrow, Mr. Hooper found himself smiling at the thought that merely a physical symbol had stood between him and joy, although the terrors it represented would forever create a dark barrier between even the most devoted lovers.

From that time forward, no one tried to remove Mr. Hooper's black veil or make a direct appeal to uncover the secret it was believed to conceal. People who considered themselves above common prejudices dismissed it as simply an odd quirk, the kind that sometimes mixes with the sensible behavior of otherwise reasonable men and colors all their actions with a hint of madness. But among the general public, good Mr. Hooper had become permanently frightening. He couldn't walk down the street with any peace of mind, knowing full well that gentle and shy people would step aside to avoid him, while others would make it a point of bravery to deliberately cross his path. The rudeness of this second group forced him to abandon his usual evening walk to the cemetery, because whenever he leaned thoughtfully against the gate, faces would always appear from behind the tombstones, staring at his black veil. A story spread around town that the gaze of the dead had driven him away from that place. It pained him deeply in his compassionate heart to see how children ran from him when he approached, abandoning their happiest games while his sorrowful figure was still far in the distance. Their natural fear made him realize more powerfully than anything else that something supernatural and terrifying was woven into the fabric of that black cloth. In fact, his own dislike of the veil was so well known that he never willingly walked past a mirror or bent down to drink from a calm spring, afraid he might be startled by his own reflection in its peaceful surface. This behavior gave credibility to the rumors that Mr. Hooper's conscience was tormenting him for some terrible crime too awful to be completely hidden, except through such dark hints. So from beneath the black veil, a shadow spread into the sunlight—an unclear mixture of sin or grief that surrounded the unfortunate minister, preventing love or compassion from ever reaching him. People said that ghosts and demons kept him company there. With inner trembling and visible fears, he walked constantly in its shadow, searching blindly within his own soul or looking at the world through something that made everything seem sad. Even the wild wind, people believed, respected his terrible secret and never blew the veil aside. Yet still, good Mr. Hooper smiled sadly at the pale faces of the worldly crowd as he walked past them.

Among all its harmful effects, the black veil had one beneficial result: it made the person wearing it an extremely effective clergyman. With the help of his mysterious symbol—since there was no other obvious reason—he became a man with tremendous power over souls who were suffering because of their sins. His converts always looked at him with a unique kind of fear, claiming, though only in a symbolic sense, that before he led them to heavenly light, they had been with him behind the black veil. The darkness of the veil actually allowed him to understand all troubled emotions. Dying sinners called out loudly for Mr. Hooper and refused to take their last breath until he came to them, though whenever he leaned down to whisper comfort, they trembled at the veiled face so close to their own. These were the fears that the black veil inspired even when Death had revealed his own face. Strangers traveled great distances to attend services at his church simply to stare at his appearance because they were forbidden from seeing his actual face. But many left feeling shaken. On one occasion, during Governor Belcher's time in office, Mr. Hooper was chosen to deliver the election sermon. Wearing his black veil, he stood before the chief magistrate, the council, and the representatives, and made such a powerful impression that the laws passed that year reflected all the somberness and religious devotion of our earliest founding leaders.

In this way, Mr. Hooper lived a long life, blameless in his public actions, yet surrounded by troubling doubts; he was kind and loving, though he remained unloved and quietly feared; he was a man isolated from others, avoided during their times of health and happiness, but always called upon to help them in their moments of dying agony. As the years passed, leaving their snows upon his black veil, he gained recognition throughout the New England churches, and they began calling him Father Hooper. Nearly all of his parishioners who had been adults when he first arrived had been carried away by countless funerals: he now had one congregation in the church and an even larger one in the cemetery; and, having worked so late into the evening and performed his duties so well, it was now good Father Hooper's time to rest.

Several people could be seen in the flickering candlelight of the old minister's death chamber. He had no family members present. But the physician was there, maintaining his professional composure while remaining emotionally detached, focused only on easing the final suffering of a patient he couldn't heal. The deacons and other deeply religious members of his congregation had gathered as well. Reverend Mr. Clark from Westbury was also present—a young and passionate clergyman who had rushed over to offer prayers at the dying minister's bedside. The nurse was there too—not some hired servant of death, but someone whose quiet devotion had lasted all these years in secret, in isolation, through the coldness of old age, and wouldn't fade even in this final hour. It was Elizabeth! And there lay the gray-haired head of good Father Hooper on his deathbed pillow, with the black veil still wrapped around his forehead and hanging down over his face, so that each labored breath he took made the fabric flutter. Throughout his entire life, that piece of black cloth had created a barrier between him and the world; it had cut him off from warm friendships and romantic love, trapping him in the loneliest prison of all—his own heart; and it still covered his face now, as if to make his dark room even gloomier and shield him from the light of eternal life.

For quite some time, his mind had been clouded and uncertain, swinging back and forth between past and present, and drifting forward at times into the vague uncertainty of what was to come. He had experienced feverish episodes that threw him from one side to the other and drained what little energy remained in him. Yet even during his most violent struggles and the wildest wanderings of his mind, when no other thought could maintain its clear influence, he continued to show a terrible concern that the black veil might slip away. Even if his confused soul might have forgotten, there was a devoted woman beside his bed who, with her eyes turned away, would have covered that elderly face which she had last seen in the beauty of his younger years.

At last, the dying old man lay still in a state of complete mental and physical exhaustion, his pulse barely detectable and his breathing growing weaker and weaker, except when a long, deep, and uneven breath seemed to signal that his spirit was about to depart.

The minister of Westbury walked over to the bedside.

"Reverend Father Hooper," he said, "the moment of your freedom is here. Are you prepared for the removal of the veil that separates time from eternity?"

Father Hooper initially responded with just a weak movement of his head; then—worried, perhaps, that his intention might be unclear—he made an effort to speak.

"Yes," he said in a weak voice; "my soul feels a patient exhaustion until that veil is lifted."

"Is it appropriate," continued Reverend Mr. Clark, "that a man so devoted to prayer, who has lived such an exemplary life, holy in both actions and thoughts, as far as human judgment can determine—is it appropriate that a church leader should leave behind a shadow on his legacy that might seem to taint such a pure life? I beg you, my respected brother, don't let this happen! Allow us to be filled with joy by your victorious appearance as you go to receive your eternal reward. Before the curtain of eternity is drawn back, let me remove this black veil from your face;" and, speaking these words, Reverend Mr. Clark leaned forward to uncover the mystery that had persisted for so many years.

But with a sudden burst of energy that left all the onlookers stunned, Father Hooper pulled both hands from under the bedcovers and pressed them firmly against the black veil, determined to fight if the minister of Westbury chose to struggle with a dying man.

"Never!" cried the veiled clergyman. "On earth, never!"

"Dark old man," cried the terrified minister, "what terrible crime weighs on your soul as you now face judgment?"

Father Hooper's breathing was labored and rattled in his throat, but with tremendous effort, he reached forward with his hands, grasped onto life, and held it back until he could speak. He even managed to sit up in bed, where he sat trembling with Death's arms wrapped around him, while the black veil hung down, terrifying in that final moment with all the accumulated fears of a lifetime. Yet the faint, melancholy smile that had so often appeared there now seemed to shine through the darkness and remain on Father Hooper's lips.

"Why do you fear me alone?" he cried out, turning his covered face toward the circle of pale onlookers. "Fear each other as well. Have people avoided me and women shown no compassion and children screamed and run away simply because of my black veil? What except the mystery that it dimly represents has made this piece of cloth so terrifying? When a friend reveals his deepest heart to his friend, the lover to his most beloved; when a person does not foolishly hide from the gaze of his Creator, disgustingly hoarding the secret of his wrongdoing—then consider me a monster for the symbol under which I have lived and will die. I look around me, and behold! on every face a black veil!"

While those listening pulled away from each other in shared terror, Father Hooper collapsed back onto his pillow, a covered corpse with a faint smile still visible on his lips. They placed him in his coffin with the veil still on, and carried him to his burial as a veiled body. The grass has grown and died many times over that grave through the years, moss now covers the headstone, and good Mr. Hooper's face has turned to dust; yet the disturbing thought remains that it decayed beneath that black veil.

The Maypole of Merry Mount

The fascinating history of the early settlement of Mount Wollaston, or Merry Mount, provides an excellent foundation for a philosophical romance. In this brief sketch that I have attempted here, the facts recorded on the serious pages of our New England historians have transformed themselves almost naturally into a kind of allegory. The masques, theatrical performances, and celebratory traditions described in the text align with the customs of that era. Documentation supporting these details can be found in Strutt's Book of English Sports and Pastimes.

The days at Merry Mount shone brightly when the Maypole served as the flagpole for that cheerful settlement. Those who raised it believed that if their banner proved victorious, they would spread sunlight across New England's rough hills and plant flower seeds throughout the land. Joy and sadness were fighting for control of a kingdom. Midsummer's eve had arrived, bringing rich green growth to the forest and roses with colors more brilliant than the delicate buds of spring. But May, or her joyful spirit, lived year-round at Merry Mount, playing with the summer months, celebrating with autumn, and warming herself by winter's fireplace. Through a world filled with hard work and worry, she moved with a dreamlike smile and came to this place to make her home among the carefree hearts of Merry Mount.

Never before had the Maypole been decorated so festively as it was at sunset on Midsummer's Eve. This revered symbol was a pine tree that had maintained the graceful elegance of youth while reaching the towering height of the ancient forest giants. From its peak flowed a silk banner painted in rainbow colors. Nearly down to the earth, the pole was adorned with birch branches and others of the most vibrant green, along with some bearing silver leaves attached by ribbons that danced in whimsical clusters of twenty different hues, though none were somber. Garden flowers and wild blossoms smiled joyfully among the greenery, appearing so fresh and moist with dew that they seemed to have sprouted by enchantment on that blessed pine tree. Where this lush and flowering magnificence ended, the trunk of the Maypole was painted with the seven vivid colors of the banner at its crown. On the lowest green branch hung a generous garland of roses—some that had been picked from the sunniest clearings of the forest, and others with an even deeper crimson, which the settlers had cultivated from English seeds. O people of the Golden Age, the primary focus of your farming was to grow flowers!

But what was the wild crowd that stood hand in hand around the Maypole? It couldn't be that the fauns and nymphs, when driven from their classical groves and homes of ancient legend, had sought refuge, as all the persecuted did, in the fresh woods of the West. These were Gothic monsters, though perhaps of Greek ancestry. On the shoulders of a handsome young man rose the head and branching antlers of a stag; a second, human in all other respects, had the grim face of a wolf; a third, still with the torso and limbs of a mortal man, showed the beard and horns of an ancient he-goat. There was the appearance of a bear standing upright, animal in all but his hind legs, which were decorated with pink silk stockings. And here, again, almost as remarkable, stood a real bear of the dark forest, offering each of his front paws to the grip of a human hand and as ready for the dance as anyone in that circle. His animal nature rose halfway to meet his companions as they bent down. Other faces wore the appearance of man or woman, but twisted or exaggerated, with red noses hanging before their mouths, which seemed of terrible depth and stretched from ear to ear in an endless fit of laughter. Here might be seen the wild man—well known in heraldry—hairy as a baboon and wrapped with green leaves. By his side—a more noble figure, but still a fake—appeared an Indian hunter with feathered headdress and wampum belt. Many of this strange company wore fool's caps and had little bells attached to their clothing, jingling with a silvery sound that responded to the silent music of their joyful spirits. Some young men and women were dressed more soberly, yet still maintained their places in the chaotic crowd by the expression of wild celebration upon their faces.

These were the settlers of Merry Mount as they gathered in the warm glow of sunset around their beloved Maypole. If a traveler lost in the gloomy forest had heard their laughter and caught a fearful glimpse, he might have imagined them as followers of Comus, some already turned into animals, some halfway between human and beast, and the rest celebrating with drunken joy that came before their transformation; but a group of Puritans who observed the scene while remaining hidden compared the masked figures to those demons and damned souls that their beliefs said inhabited the dark wilderness.

Within the circle of monsters appeared the two most graceful figures that had ever walked on anything more solid than a purple-and-golden cloud. One was a young man in shimmering clothing with a rainbow-patterned scarf draped across his chest. His right hand held a golden staff—the symbol of high rank among the celebrants—and his left hand clasped the delicate fingers of a beautiful young woman dressed just as festively as he was. Brilliant roses glowed against the dark and shining curls of both their heads, and the flowers were scattered around their feet or had bloomed naturally there. Behind this cheerful pair, standing so close to the Maypole that its branches cast shadows over his merry face, stood an English priest in traditional religious robes, yet adorned with flowers in pagan style and wearing a crown of native vine leaves. From the wild look in his rolling eyes and the heathen decorations on his sacred clothing, he appeared to be the most untamed creature there, the very embodiment of Comus leading the group.

"Followers of the Maypole," called out the flower-adorned priest, "all day long the woods have joyfully echoed with your laughter and celebration. But let this be your most joyful hour, my dear friends! Look! Here stand the Lord and Lady of the May, whom I, a scholar from Oxford and high priest of Merry Mount, am about to unite in holy marriage. Lift up your lively spirits, you morris dancers, green men and cheerful maidens, bears and wolves and horned gentlemen! Come! Let us have a chorus now, rich with the ancient joy of Merry England and the wilder happiness of this fresh forest, and then a dance, to show the young couple what life is made of and how lightly they should move through it! All you who love the Maypole, raise your voices to the wedding song of the Lord and Lady of the May!"

This marriage was more meaningful than most celebrations at Merry Mount, where jokes and illusions, pranks and imagination, maintained a constant festival atmosphere. The Lord and Lady of the May, although they would have to give up their titles at sunset, were genuinely going to be companions for life's dance, starting their rhythm that very bright evening. The garland of roses hanging from the lowest green branch of the Maypole had been woven for them, and would be placed over both their heads as a symbol of their blossoming union. When the priest finished speaking, therefore, a wild celebration erupted from the crowd of bizarre figures.

"Start the song, reverend sir," they all shouted, "and never have the woods echoed with such a joyful sound as we at the Maypole will create."

Instantly, a musical introduction featuring pipe, cittern, and viol, played with skilled musicianship, started from a nearby grove of trees with such a joyful rhythm that the branches of the Maypole trembled from the sound. However, the May-lord—the one carrying the golden staff—happening to gaze into his lady's eyes, was amazed by the almost thoughtful look that met his own.

"Edith, sweet Lady of the May," he whispered with reproach, "is that wreath of roses meant to be a garland for our graves that you appear so sorrowful? Oh, Edith, this is our golden moment. Don't let any melancholy thoughts cloud it, because it's possible that nothing in our future will shine brighter than simply remembering what we're experiencing right now."

"That exact thought was what made me sad. How did it come to your mind as well?" Edith said, speaking even more quietly than he was, because feeling sad at Merry Mount was considered a serious offense. "That's why I'm sighing despite all this celebratory music. And also, dear Edgar, I feel like I'm fighting against a dream, imagining that these figures of our cheerful friends are just illusions and their happiness isn't real, and that we aren't truly the lord and lady of the May. What is this mystery I feel in my heart?"

At that very moment, as though some enchantment had released them, a small cascade of wilted rose petals drifted down from the Maypole. How tragic for the young couple in love! The instant their hearts burned with genuine passion, they became aware of something hollow and insubstantial in their previous joys, and experienced a melancholy foreboding of unavoidable change. From the moment they truly fell in love, they had bound themselves to earth's fate of worry and grief and anxious happiness, and no longer belonged at Merry Mount. That was Edith's secret. Now let us leave the priest to wed them, and the costumed revelers to celebrate around the Maypole until the final ray of sunlight disappears from its peak and the forest's shadows blend darkly into the dance. In the meantime, we might learn who these cheerful people actually were.

Two centuries ago, and even longer, the Old World and its people grew tired of each other. Thousands of men sailed west—some to trade glass and similar trinkets for furs from Indian hunters, some to conquer untouched empires, and one determined group to worship. But none of these reasons carried much influence with the settlers of Merry Mount. Their leaders were men who had played with life for so long that when Thought and Wisdom arrived, even these unwanted visitors were led astray by the multitude of frivolities they should have driven away. Misguided Thought and corrupted Wisdom were forced to wear masks and act like fools. The men we're discussing, after losing their heart's natural joy, conceived a reckless philosophy of pleasure and came here to live out their latest fantasy. They attracted followers from all those lightheaded people whose entire existence resembles the celebration days of more serious men. Among their company were musicians, well-known on London's streets; traveling actors whose stages had been the halls of aristocrats; performers, tightrope walkers, and charlatans who would be greatly missed at festivals, church celebrations, and markets; in short, entertainers of every kind, who were plentiful in that era but were now beginning to be discouraged by Puritanism's rapid expansion. Their steps had been light on land, and just as lightly they crossed the ocean. Many had been driven to cheerful desperation by their past hardships; others were equally wild in their youth's excitement, like the May Lord and his Lady; but whatever the nature of their joy might be, both old and young were merry at Merry Mount. The young believed themselves content. The older souls, if they understood that merriment was merely happiness's imitation, still chased the false illusion deliberately, because at least its clothing sparkled most brightly. Lifelong devotees of trivial pursuits, they refused to venture among life's serious realities, not even to find true blessing.

All the traditional celebrations of Old England were brought to this new land. The King of Christmas received his proper coronation, and the Lord of Misrule held powerful authority. On St. John's Eve, they cut down entire acres of forest to build bonfires, dancing around the flames throughout the night while wearing flower crowns and tossing blossoms into the fire. During harvest season, even though their crops were quite small, they created a figure from bundles of Indian corn, decorated it with autumn wreaths, and carried it home in celebration. However, what most distinguished the settlers of Merry Mount was their deep reverence for the Maypole. This devotion transformed their actual history into something resembling a poet's story. Spring adorned the sacred symbol with fresh flowers and new green branches; Summer contributed roses in the richest crimson and the forest's fully developed leaves; Autumn enhanced it with brilliant reds and yellows that turned every wild leaf into a colorful blossom; and Winter coated it with ice and surrounded it with icicles until it sparkled in the cold sunlight like a frozen ray of light. In this way, each changing season honored the Maypole and offered it the finest beauty it possessed. The devoted followers danced around it at least once every month; sometimes they called it their faith or their sacred place; but it always served as the ceremonial pole of Merry Mount.

Unfortunately, there were men in the new world who held a much stricter faith than those who celebrated around the Maypole. Close to Merry Mount stood a Puritan settlement, filled with the most somber people, who recited their prayers before dawn and then labored in the forest or cornfields until evening brought prayer time once more. They kept their weapons ready at all times to strike down any wandering native. When they gathered together, it was never to maintain the traditional English merriment, but to listen to sermons that lasted three hours, or to announce rewards for wolf heads and Indian scalps. Their celebrations were days of fasting, and their primary entertainment was singing psalms. Pity the young man or woman who even dared to dream of dancing! The selectman would signal to the constable, and there the nimble-footed sinner would sit locked in the stocks; or if he did dance, it would be around the whipping-post, which could be called the Puritan Maypole.

A group of these stern Puritans, struggling through the challenging woods, each carrying a horse's load of iron armor that weighed down their steps, would sometimes approach the bright boundaries of Merry Mount. There were the well-dressed colonists, frolicking around their Maypole; perhaps training a bear to dance, or trying to share their joy with the serious Indian, or dressing up in the skins of deer and wolves that they had hunted specifically for this

33

purpose. Often the entire colony was playing Blindman's Buff, magistrates and everyone else with their eyes covered, except for a single target, whom the blindfolded sinners chased by following the jingling of the bells on his clothes. Once, it is said, they were seen following a flower-covered corpse with joy and celebratory music to his burial. But did the dead man laugh? In their calmest moments they sang songs and shared stories for the enlightenment of their religious visitors, or confused them with magic tricks, or made faces at them through horse-collars; and when entertainment itself became tiresome, they mocked their own foolishness and started a yawning contest. At even the smallest of these outrages the iron-clad men shook their heads and scowled so deeply that the celebrants looked up, thinking that a brief cloud had blocked the sunshine that was supposed to last forever there. On the other hand, the Puritans declared that when a psalm echoed from their place of worship, the response that the forest returned to them often sounded like the refrain of a cheerful song, ending with a burst of laughter. Who but the devil and his servants, the people of Merry Mount, could have disturbed them this way? Eventually a conflict developed, harsh and bitter on one side, and as earnest on the other as anything could be among such carefree spirits who had pledged loyalty to the Maypole. The future character of New England depended on this significant dispute. Should the somber saints establish their authority over the joyful sinners, then their mood would darken the entire region and make it a land of gloomy faces, of hard labor, of sermons and psalms forever; but should the flagpole of Merry Mount prove victorious, sunshine would shine upon the hills, and flowers would adorn the forest and future generations would pay tribute to the Maypole.

After these genuine historical accounts, we return to the wedding of the Lord and Lady of the May. Unfortunately, we have waited too long and must darken our story too abruptly. As we look once more at the Maypole, a single sunbeam is disappearing from the top, leaving only a pale golden glow mixed with the colors of the rainbow banner. Even that faint light is now gone, giving up the entire territory of Merry Mount to the evening darkness that has swept so suddenly from the black surrounding forest. But some of these dark shadows have emerged in human form.

Yes, as the sun set, the final day of celebration had ended at Merry Mount. The circle of cheerful costumed revelers was scattered and broken; the stag hung his antlers in defeat; the wolf became weaker than a lamb; the bells of the folk dancers jingled with fearful trembling. The Puritans had played their typical role in the Maypole festivities. Their dark figures were mixed among the wild forms of their enemies, creating a scene that resembled the moment when conscious thoughts emerge among the fading remnants of a dream. The leader of the opposing group stood at the center of the circle, while the crowd of costumed figures crouched around him like evil spirits before a fearsome sorcerer. No playful nonsense could meet his gaze. His presence was so intensely stern that his entire being—face, body, and spirit—seemed forged from iron given life and consciousness, yet made of the same material as his helmet and armor. This was the Puritan among Puritans: this was Endicott himself.

"Get away, priest of Baal!" he said, with a fierce scowl and placing no respectful hand upon the vestment. "I know you, Blackstone! You are the man who could not tolerate the authority even of your own corrupt Church, and have come here to preach wickedness and to demonstrate it through your life. But now it shall be seen that the Lord has made this wilderness sacred for his chosen people. Woe to those who would corrupt it! And first for this flower-adorned abomination, the altar of your worship!"[2]

With his sharp sword, Endicott attacked the sacred Maypole. It didn't withstand his assault for long. The pole groaned with a mournful sound, scattering leaves and rosebuds onto the relentless zealot, and finally, with all its green branches and ribbons and flowers that symbolized lost joys, the flagpole of Merry Mount came crashing down. As it fell, legend tells us, the evening sky grew gloomier and the forest cast a darker shadow.

"There!" shouted Endicott, gazing triumphantly at what he had accomplished; "there lies the only Maypole in New England. I am deeply convinced that its destruction foreshadows the destiny of frivolous and carefree revelers among us and our descendants. Amen, says John Endicott!"

"Amen!" echoed his followers.

But the followers of the Maypole let out a single groan for their beloved symbol. At that sound, the Puritan leader looked at the group of revelers, each one normally full of joyful laughter, yet now strangely showing expressions of sadness and alarm.

"Brave captain," said Peter Palfrey, the veteran of the group, "what should we do with the prisoners?"

"I didn't think I would regret cutting down a Maypole," Endicott replied, "but now I find myself wanting to put it back up and let each of these savage heathens have one more dance around their idol. It would have made an excellent whipping post."

"But there are plenty of pine trees," the lieutenant suggested.

"You're right, good elder," said the leader. "Therefore tie up the pagan crew and give each of them a few lashes as a preview of the justice we'll deliver later. Put some of these criminals in the stocks to wait once Providence brings us to one of our own well-organized settlements where such facilities can be found. Additional punishments, such as branding and cutting off ears, will be considered afterward."

"How many lashes should the priest receive?" asked Ancient Palfrey.

"Not yet," Endicott replied, fixing his stern glare on the offender. "The Great and General Court must decide whether whipping and lengthy imprisonment, along with other severe punishments, can make up for his crimes. He should watch himself carefully. We might show mercy to those who break our civil laws, but disaster awaits anyone who disrupts our religion!"

"And what about this dancing bear?" the officer continued. "Should he receive the same punishment as his companions?"

"Shoot him through the head!" said the energetic Puritan. "I suspect witchcraft in the beast."

"Here are a couple of radiant ones," Peter Palfrey continued, pointing his weapon at the Lord and Lady of the May. "They appear to be of high rank among these wrongdoers. I believe their status will require nothing less than a double portion of lashes."

Endicott leaned on his sword and carefully examined the clothing and appearance of the unfortunate couple. There they stood, pale, dejected, and fearful, yet there was a quality of mutual support and pure love seeking help and offering it that revealed them to be husband and wife with a priest's blessing upon their union. The young man, in the danger of the moment, had dropped his decorated staff and wrapped his arm around the Lady of the May, who rested against his chest too gently to weigh him down, but with enough pressure to show that their fates were bound together for better or worse. They looked first at each other and then into the stern captain's face. There they stood in the first hour of marriage, while the carefree pleasures that their companions represented had been replaced by life's harshest responsibilities, embodied by the somber Puritans. But never had their youthful beauty appeared so pure and noble as when its radiance was tempered by hardship.

"Young man," said Endicott, "you find yourself in a terrible situation—both you and your new bride. Get ready immediately, because I intend for both of you to have something to remember your wedding day by."

"Harsh man," shouted the May-lord, "how can I persuade you? If I had the means available, I would fight to the death; since I'm powerless, I beg you. Do whatever you want with me, but leave Edith unharmed."

"Not so," replied the relentless zealot. "We don't usually show empty courtesy to that sex which requires stricter discipline. What do you say, girl? Should your pampered bridegroom suffer your share of the punishment in addition to his own?"

"Let it be death," said Edith, "and put it all on me."

Indeed, as Endicott had observed, the unfortunate lovers found themselves in a terrible situation. Their enemies had won, their allies were imprisoned and humiliated, their home lay in ruins, the dark wilderness surrounded them, and their sole guide was a harsh fate embodied by the Puritan leader. Still, the growing dusk couldn't completely hide the fact that this stern man had been moved. He smiled at the beautiful sight of young love;

he nearly mourned for the certain destruction of youthful dreams.

"Life's hardships have arrived quickly for this young couple," Endicott remarked. "We'll observe how they handle their current challenges before we impose heavier burdens on them. If there are any more respectable clothes among the confiscated items, have them dress this May-lord and his Lady instead of their flashy finery. See to it, some of you."

"And shouldn't the young man's hair be cut?" asked Peter Palfrey, looking with disgust at the love-lock and long shiny curls of the youth.

"Cut it down immediately, and do it in the proper way," the captain replied. "Then bring them with us, but treat them more gently than we treated the others. The young man has qualities that could make him brave in battle, dedicated in work, and devout in prayer, and the young woman has traits that could help her become a mother in our community, raising children with better guidance than she herself received. Don't think, young people, that those who waste their brief lives dancing around a Maypole are the happiest, even during our short time on earth."

And Endicott, the most rigid Puritan of all those who established the foundation of New England, picked up the wreath of roses from the destroyed Maypole and threw it with his own armored hand over the heads of the Lord and Lady of the May. This act carried prophetic meaning. Just as the moral darkness of the world overwhelms all organized celebration, their place of unbridled joy became empty within the somber forest. They never returned to it again. But just as their flower garland was woven from the most beautiful roses that had bloomed there, the bond that joined them together contained all the most innocent and finest elements of their youthful happiness. They walked toward heaven, supporting one another along the challenging path they were destined to follow, and never spent a single moment regretting the empty pleasures of Merry Mount.

The Gentle Boy

In 1656, several people known as Quakers—guided, as they claimed, by the inner movement of the spirit—arrived in New England. Their reputation as believers in mystical and dangerous ideas had preceded them, so the Puritans quickly tried to exile them and prevent further infiltration by this emerging religious group. However, the actions intended to cleanse the land of heresy, while more than harsh enough, proved completely ineffective. The Quakers viewed persecution as a divine calling to positions of danger and claimed to possess a sacred bravery that the Puritans themselves lacked, since the Puritans had avoided suffering by establishing their religion's peaceful practice in a remote wilderness. Although it was remarkable that every nation on earth rejected these wandering religious enthusiasts who practiced peace toward all people, the location of greatest hostility and danger, and thus the most appealing to them, was the Massachusetts Bay colony.

The fines, imprisonments, and beatings generously handed out by our devout ancestors, along with the widespread public hatred that lasted nearly a century after the actual persecution had ended, served as powerful attractions for the Quakers—just as peace, honor, and rewards would have appealed to those focused on worldly concerns. Every ship from Europe brought fresh groups of sect members, eager to bear witness against the oppression they hoped to experience themselves; and when ship captains were prevented from giving them passage due to heavy penalties, they undertook long and roundabout journeys through Indian territory, appearing in the province as though transported by some divine force. Their fervor, intensified almost to the point of insanity by the treatment they endured, led to behaviors that violated both standards of propriety and rational religious practice, creating a striking contrast to the calm and steady conduct of their present-day sectarian descendants. The Spirit's command, which could only be heard by the soul and could not be challenged through human reasoning, became justification for highly inappropriate displays that, viewed objectively, certainly warranted the mild punishment of physical discipline. These excesses, along with the persecution that was simultaneously their cause and result, continued to escalate until 1659, when the Massachusetts Bay government granted two members of the Quaker sect the honor of martyrdom.

An permanent stain of blood marks the hands of everyone who agreed to this action, but a significant portion of the terrible responsibility must fall upon the person who was leading the government at that time. He was a man with a limited mind and incomplete education, and his inflexible prejudice was intensified and made dangerous by violent and rash emotions; he used his power inappropriately and without justification to bring about the death of these zealots, and his entire behavior toward them was characterized by savage cruelty. The Quakers, whose vengeful emotions were no less profound because they remained unexpressed, remembered this man and his companions in later years. The historian of the religious group claims that through divine anger a curse fell upon the land surrounding the "bloody town" of Boston, making it impossible for wheat to grow there; and he positions himself, as it were, among the burial sites of the old persecutors, and victoriously describes the punishments that befell them in their old age or at the moment of death. He tells us that they died suddenly and violently and in insanity, but nothing can surpass the harsh ridicule with which he documents the disgusting illness and "death by decay" of the savage and merciless governor.

On the evening of the autumn day that had witnessed the execution of two Quaker men, a Puritan settler was making his way back from the city to the nearby country town where he lived. The air was crisp, the sky was clear, and the fading twilight grew brighter from the light of a young moon that had almost reached the edge of the horizon. The traveler, a middle-aged man wearing a gray wool cloak, picked up his pace once he reached the town's outskirts, since a dark stretch of nearly four miles stretched between him and his home. The low houses with straw roofs were spread far apart along the road, and because the area had been settled for only about thirty years, patches of original forest still made up a significant portion compared to the farmed land. The autumn wind drifted through the branches, spinning the leaves away from all the trees except the pines and moaning as though it mourned the destruction it caused. The road had cut through the mass of woods closest to the town and was just opening into a clearing when the traveler heard a sound more sorrowful than even the wind. It sounded like someone crying in anguish, and it appeared to come from beneath a tall and isolated fir tree standing in the center of a cleared but unfenced and unfarmed field. The Puritan couldn't help but recall that this was the exact location that had been cursed just a few hours earlier by the execution of the Quakers, whose bodies had been hastily buried together in a single grave beneath the tree where they had died. Still, he fought against the superstitious fears common to that time and forced himself to stop and listen.

"The voice is probably human, and I have no reason to be afraid even if it isn't," he thought, peering through the faint moonlight. "I think it sounds like a child crying—perhaps some baby that has wandered away from its mother and ended up in this place of death. For my own peace of mind, I need to investigate this." He left the path and walked somewhat nervously across the field. Though it was now so empty, the ground was packed down and trampled by the thousands of footsteps of those who had witnessed today's spectacle, all of whom had gone home, leaving the dead alone.

The traveler finally reached the fir tree, which was covered with living branches from its middle section upward, though a scaffold had been built underneath it, along with other preparations for carrying out an execution. Beneath this cursed tree—which people in later years would believe dripped poison with its morning dew—sat the only person mourning for innocent blood that had been spilled. It was a thin, lightly dressed little boy who pressed his face against a mound of freshly dug and partially frozen soil, crying intensely but quietly, as though expressing his sorrow might itself be punished as a crime. The Puritan, who had approached without being noticed, placed his hand on the child's shoulder and spoke to him with kindness.

"You've picked a gloomy place to stay, my poor boy, and it's no surprise that you're crying," he said. "But wipe away your tears and tell me where your mother lives; I promise you, if the journey isn't too far, I'll have you back in her arms tonight."

The boy immediately stopped crying and looked up at the stranger. His face was pale with bright eyes, clearly no older than six, but sadness, fear, and hardship had stripped away much of his childlike innocence. The Puritan noticed the boy's terrified stare and felt him shaking beneath his touch, so he tried to comfort him:

"No, if I wanted to hurt you, young boy, the easiest thing would be to leave you right here. What! You're not afraid to sit under the gallows on a freshly dug grave, yet you shake when a friend touches you? Be brave, child, and tell me your name and where you live."

"Friend," the little boy replied in a sweet but trembling voice, "they call me Ilbrahim, and my home is here."

The pale, otherworldly face, the eyes that appeared to blend with the moonlight, the gentle, ethereal voice and the strange name nearly convinced the Puritan that the boy was actually a spirit that had risen from the grave where he sat; but noticing that the vision withstood a brief silent prayer, and recalling that the arm he had touched felt real and warm, he came to a more logical conclusion. "The poor child has lost his mind," he thought, "but truly his words are disturbing in a place such as this." He then spoke gently, planning to go along with the boy's delusion:

"Your home will hardly be comfortable, Ilbrahim, on this cold autumn night, and I'm afraid you don't have enough food. I'm hurrying to a warm supper and bed, and if you come with me, you can share them."

"Thank you, friend, but even though I'm hungry and shivering from the cold, you won't give me food or shelter," the boy replied in the quiet tone that despair had taught him despite his young age. "My father was one of the people that everyone hates; they've buried him under this pile of earth, and this is my home."

The Puritan, who had taken hold of little Ilbrahim's hand, let it go as if he were touching a disgusting snake.

However, he had a kind heart that even religious bias couldn't turn to stone. "God forbid that I should abandon this child to die, even though he belongs to that cursed group," he said to himself. "Don't we all come from a sinful beginning? Aren't we all lost in darkness until the light shines on us? He won't die, not in body, and if prayer and teaching can help him, not in soul either." He then spoke out loud and gently to Ilbrahim, who had once again buried his face in the cold dirt of the grave:

"Was every door in the country closed to you, my child, that you have come to this cursed place?"

"They forced me out of the prison when they took my father away," the boy said, "and I stood at a distance watching the crowd of people; and after they left, I came here, and found only this grave. I knew that my father was resting here, and I said, 'This will be my home.'"

"No, child, no, not while I have a roof over my head or a bite of food to share with you," declared the Puritan, whose compassion was now completely stirred. "Get up and come with me, and don't be afraid of any harm."

The boy began crying again and held tightly to the mound of dirt as though the lifeless heart buried beneath it offered him more warmth than any beating heart in a living person. The traveler, though, kept gently pleading with him, and appearing to gain some measure of trust, the boy finally stood up; however, his thin limbs shook with frailty, his small head became lightheaded, and he rested against the tree of death to steady himself.

"My poor boy, are you so weak?" said the Puritan. "When did you last eat?"

"I shared bread and water with my father in prison," Ibrahim answered, "but they haven't brought him any food yesterday or today, claiming he had eaten enough to sustain him until his journey's end. Don't worry about my hunger, kind friend, because I've gone without food many times before."

The traveler lifted the child into his arms and wrapped his cloak around him, his heart filling with shame and anger at the needless cruelty of those carrying out this persecution. As his emotions awakened, he decided that no matter what dangers he might face, he would not abandon this poor, helpless child whom Heaven had placed in his care. With this resolve, he left the cursed field and returned to the homeward path from which the boy's crying had drawn him away. The light and still burden barely slowed his steps, and soon he could see the firelight glowing from the windows of the cottage that he, a man from a faraway land, had built in the Western wilderness. The dwelling was surrounded by a large area of farmland and nestled in the shelter of a wooded hill, where it seemed to have settled for safety.

"Look up, child," the Puritan said to Ilbrahim, whose weak head had dropped onto his shoulder; "there is our home."

At the word "home" a surge of excitement ran through the child's body, but he remained quiet. Within moments they reached the cottage door, where the owner knocked; during that early time, when hostile natives roamed freely among the colonists, locks and bars were essential for protecting a home. The knock was answered by an indentured servant, a roughly dressed and plain-looking man, who, after confirming that his master was the one requesting entry, unlocked the door and held up a blazing pine torch to illuminate his way inside. Further down the hallway the red glow revealed a motherly woman, but no small group of children came rushing out to welcome their father home.

As the Puritan walked in, he pushed his cloak to one side and revealed Ilbrahim's face to the woman.

"Dorothy, here's a little outcast that Providence has placed in our care," he said. "Be kind to him, just as if he were one of those dear ones we've lost."

"Who is this pale, bright-eyed little boy, Tobias?" she asked. "Is he someone the wilderness people have taken from a Christian mother?"

"No, Dorothy; this poor child isn't a captive from the wilderness," he responded. "The heathen savage would have shared his meager meal and offered him drink from his birch cup, but Christian men, sadly, had abandoned him to die." Then he explained how he had discovered him beneath the gallows, on his father's grave, and how his heart had urged him like the voice of an inner calling to bring the little outcast home and show him kindness. He admitted his determination to feed and clothe him as though he were his own child, and to provide him with the education that would counter the harmful misconceptions that had been planted in his young mind up to this point.

Dorothy possessed an even more immediate compassion than her husband, and she supported all his actions and plans.

"Do you have a mother, dear child?" she asked.

The tears poured from his overflowing heart as he tried to respond, but Dorothy eventually realized that he had a mother who, like others in her religious group, was a persecuted exile. She had been removed from jail just a short while earlier, taken into the empty wilderness and abandoned there to die from starvation or wild animals. This was a typical way of getting rid of the Quakers, and they often took pride in saying that the creatures of the desert treated them with more kindness than civilized people did.

"Don't be afraid, little boy; you won't need a mother, and a loving one at that," Dorothy said after she had learned this information. "Wipe away your tears, Ilbrahim, and become my child, just as I will become your mother."

The kind woman prepared the small bed that had once held her own children before they were carried away to their final resting place. Before Ilbrahim agreed to sleep in it, he knelt down, and as Dorothy listened to his innocent and touching prayer, she wondered how the parents who had taught him such words could have been considered deserving of death. After the boy had drifted off to sleep, she leaned over his pale and gentle face, kissed his white forehead, pulled the blankets up around his neck, and left the room with a thoughtful joy filling her heart.

Tobias Pearson wasn't among the first settlers to leave England for the New World. He had stayed in England during the early years of the Civil War, where he served as a cavalry officer under Cromwell. However, when his leader's ambitious plans began to unfold, he left the Parliamentary army and sought refuge from what was no longer a holy conflict among his fellow believers in the Massachusetts colony. A more practical consideration may have also influenced his decision to come to America, since New England offered opportunities to men of modest means as well as to those dissatisfied with religious matters, and Pearson had struggled to support his wife and growing family. The more fanatical Puritans were inclined to blame this supposed impure motive for the deaths of all his children, for whose material welfare the father had been overly concerned. The children had left their homeland healthy and beautiful like roses, and like roses they had died in foreign soil. Those interpreters of God's will, who had judged their fellow believer this way and blamed his family tragedies on his sin, showed no more kindness when they saw him and Dorothy trying to heal the emptiness in their hearts by adopting a child from the despised Quaker sect. They made sure to express their disapproval to Tobias, but he simply responded by pointing to the small, peaceful, beautiful boy, whose appearance and behavior were indeed the strongest arguments that could possibly have been made in his favor. Even his beauty and charming ways, however, sometimes had an ultimately negative effect; for the religious extremists, after the hard surfaces of their iron hearts had been softened and then hardened again, declared that no natural cause alone could have affected them so deeply. Their hostility toward the poor child was also strengthened by the failure of various religious debates in which they tried to convince him that his sect was wrong. Ilbrahim, it's true, wasn't a skilled debater, but his religious feelings ran as deep as instinct, and he could neither be tempted nor forced to abandon the faith for which his father had died.

The hatred directed at this stubborn behavior was largely shared by the child's guardians, so much so that Tobias and Dorothy soon found themselves facing a particularly harsh form of persecution through the cold treatment they received from many friends they had cherished. The ordinary citizens expressed their views more directly. Pearson held a position of some importance, serving as a representative to the General Court and holding the rank of approved lieutenant in the local militia, yet within a week of taking in Ilbrahim, he had been both hissed at and jeered. On one occasion, while walking through an isolated stretch of forest, he heard a loud voice from an unseen speaker that called out, "What shall be done to the backslider? Look! the whip is prepared for him, even the lash of nine cords, and every cord bears three knots." These insults angered Pearson in the moment; they also penetrated his heart, becoming invisible yet potent forces working toward an outcome that his most private thoughts had not yet acknowledged.

On the second Sunday after Ilbrahim joined their household, Pearson and his wife felt it was appropriate for him to accompany them to church services. They had expected the boy might resist this plan, but he got ready quietly, and when the time came, he was dressed in the new black mourning clothes that Dorothy had made for him. Since the parish had no bell at that time, and wouldn't for many years to come, a drumbeat served as the signal for worship to begin. When the first sound of that military-style call to the place of sacred and peaceful reflection rang out, Tobias and Dorothy departed, each taking one of little Ilbrahim's hands, like two parents connected by the child they cherished. As they walked through the bare winter woods, many people they knew caught up with them, but all of these acquaintances avoided the family and crossed to the opposite side of the path. However, a more severe test of their determination awaited them when they came down the hill and approached the simple pine-constructed church building without any decorative features. Gathered around the entrance, where the drummer continued to send out his booming call, stood an intimidating formation that included several of the congregation's eldest members, many middle-aged parishioners, and almost all the younger men. Pearson struggled to endure their collective disapproving stares, but

Dorothy, whose mindset was different, simply pulled the boy closer to her side and continued forward without hesitation. As they walked through the doorway, they caught fragments of the crowd's whispered comments, and when the harsh voices of the small children reached Ilbrahim's ears, tears began to flow down his face.

The inside of the meeting house was plain and rough. The low ceiling, bare walls, exposed wooden beams, and uncovered pulpit provided nothing to inspire the religious feeling that often lies dormant in people's hearts without such visual encouragement. The floor of the building was filled with rows of long benches without cushions, taking the place of pews, and the wide center aisle created a separation between men and women that could only be crossed by children under a certain age.

Pearson and Dorothy parted ways at the entrance to the meeting house, and Ilbrahim, still being a young child, remained in Dorothy's care. The wrinkled old women wrapped themselves tightly in their worn cloaks as he walked past; even the gentle-looking young women appeared to fear being tainted by him; and many a harsh elderly man stood up and turned his cold, ungodly face toward the innocent boy, as though his very presence defiled the sacred space. He was like a pure child of heaven who had wandered far from his home, and all the people of this wretched world shut their corrupt hearts against him, pulled back their dirt-stained clothing from his touch and declared, "We are holier than thou."

Ibrahim, sitting beside his adoptive mother while holding tightly to her hand, took on a serious and respectful manner like someone mature and wise who finds himself in a temple devoted to a religion he doesn't understand but feels he should honor. The service hadn't started yet when

something seemingly unimportant caught the boy's attention. A woman with her face hidden by a hood and completely wrapped in a cloak walked slowly up the wide aisle and sat down on the front bench. Ibrahim's pale complexion changed color, his nerves trembled; he couldn't look away from the covered woman.

When the opening prayer and hymn concluded, the minister stood up and, after turning the hourglass that sat beside the large Bible, began his sermon. He was now advanced in age, a man with a pale, gaunt face, and his gray hair was completely covered by a black velvet cap. In his younger years, he had experienced firsthand what persecution meant under Archbishop Laud, and he was not inclined to forget the lesson he had once protested against. Bringing up the frequently debated topic of the Quakers, he presented a history of that religious group and described their beliefs in a way where mistakes overshadowed facts and bias twisted the truth of what was accurate. He referenced the recent actions taken in the province and warned his listeners who were less discerning against questioning the rightful harshness that God-fearing officials had finally been forced to impose. He discussed the danger of compassion—in some situations a praiseworthy and Christian quality, but not suitable for this harmful sect. He noted that their wicked stubbornness in their false beliefs was so strong that even the small children, the nursing infants, had become hardened and hopeless heretics. He declared that no person should try to convert them without Heaven's special permission, for fear that while trying to help pull them out of their spiritual pit, he himself might be thrown into its deepest parts.

The second hour was mostly over when the serm ended. An approving murmur followed, and the min

having announced a hymn, sat down feeling quite pleased with himself and tried to gauge the impact of his speech by studying the faces of his congregation. But while voices throughout the church were preparing to sing, something happened that, although not particularly uncommon during that time in the province, had never occurred before in this parish.

The veiled woman, who had remained completely still in the front row of the audience until now, stood up and climbed the pulpit stairs with slow, dignified, and steady steps. The tentative sounds of beginning harmony fell silent, and the minister sat in speechless and nearly terrified shock as she opened the door and took her place in the sacred pulpit from which his curses had just thundered forth. She then removed her cloak and hood, revealing herself in the most unusual clothing. A formless robe made of rough burlap was tied around her waist with a knotted rope; her black hair hung down over her shoulders, and its darkness was marred by pale streaks of ashes that she had scattered on her head. Her eyebrows, dark and sharply defined, intensified the deathly paleness of a face that, wasted by hunger and wild with religious fervor and strange grief, showed no hint of former beauty. This figure stood staring intently at the audience, and there was no sound or movement except for a slight trembling that everyone noticed in those around them, though they were barely aware of it in themselves. Finally, when her moment of divine inspiration arrived, she spoke for the first few minutes in a quiet voice with words that weren't always clearly spoken. Her speech showed evidence of an imagination hopelessly tangled with her reasoning; it was a vague and incomprehensible outpouring that, nevertheless, seemed to create its own atmosphere around the listener's

soul, and moved their emotions through some power unrelated to the actual words. As she continued, beautiful but unclear images would sometimes appear like bright objects moving in muddy water, or a powerful and strangely formed idea would leap forward and immediately grip either the mind or the heart. But the flow of her otherworldly eloquence soon brought her to the persecution of her religious group, and from there it was only a short step to her own particular sufferings. She was by nature a woman of intense emotions, and hatred and revenge now clothed themselves in the appearance of religious devotion. The nature of her speech transformed; her images became clear though wild, and her condemnations carried an almost demonic bitterness.

"The governor and his powerful men," she said, "have come together, discussing among themselves and saying, 'What should we do to these people—to the people who have come to this land to expose our wrongdoing?' And look! The devil enters the council chamber like a limping man of short height, dressed formally, with a dark and twisted face and a bright, downcast eye. And he stands up among the rulers; yes, he moves back and forth, whispering to each one; and every man listens closely, because his message is 'Kill! Kill!' But I tell you, disaster awaits those who kill! Disaster awaits those who spill the blood of saints! Disaster awaits those who have murdered the husband and thrown out the child, the helpless infant, to wander without a home, hungry and cold until he dies, and have kept the mother alive through the cruelty of their false mercy! Disaster awaits them in their lifetime! Cursed are they in the joy and pleasure of their hearts! Disaster awaits them in their final hour, whether it comes quickly with blood and violence or after long and lingering pain! Disaster in the dark house, in the decay of the grave, when the children's children will curse the ashes of their ancestors! Disaster, disaster, disaster, at the judgment, when all the persecuted and all the murdered in this bloody land, and the father, the mother and the child, will be waiting for them on a day they cannot escape! Children of the faith, children of the faith, you whose hearts are stirring with a power you do not understand, rise up, cleanse your hands of this innocent blood! Raise your voices, chosen ones, cry out loudly, and call down disaster and judgment with me!"

After releasing this flood of spite that she mistook for divine inspiration, the speaker fell silent. Her voice was replaced by the hysterical screams of several women, but the feelings of the audience as a whole had not been swept along with her current. They remained stunned, left stranded, so to speak, in the middle of a torrent that deafened them with its roar but could not move them through its force. The clergyman, who until now could not have removed the intruder from his pulpit except through physical force, now spoke to her with a tone of righteous anger and proper authority.

"Get down from this holy place that you're defiling," he said. "Is this really why you've come to the Lord's house—to spill out the corruption from your heart and the devil's influence? Get down from there, and remember that you've been sentenced to death—yes, and that sentence will be carried out, if only for what you've done today."

"I'm leaving, friend, I'm leaving, because the voice has spoken what it needed to say," she replied in a dejected and even gentle tone. "I have completed my mission to you and your people; punish me with beatings, imprisonment, or death, as you are allowed to do." The weakness from her drained emotions made her steps unsteady as she walked down the pulpit stairs.

Meanwhile, the people were moving around on the floor of the house, whispering among themselves and looking toward the intruder. Many of them now recognized her as the woman who had attacked the governor with terrible language as he walked past the window of her prison; they also knew that she had been sentenced to death, and had been spared only through an unwilling exile into the wilderness. The recent offense that had brought about her fate seemed to make any further mercy impossible, and a gentleman in military uniform, along with a sturdy man of lower rank, moved toward the door of the meetinghouse and waited for her to approach. Her feet had barely touched the floor, however, when an unexpected scene unfolded. In that moment of her danger, when every eye glared with death, a small frightened boy threw his arms around his mother.

"I'm here, mother; it's me, and I'll go with you to prison," he exclaimed.

She looked at him with uncertainty and fear in her eyes, because she knew the boy had been abandoned to die, and she hadn't expected to see him alive again. She worried that this might just be another joyful illusion that her troubled mind had created during her lonely time in the wilderness or while imprisoned; but when she felt the warmth of his hand in hers and listened to his sweet words of innocent love, she started to realize that she was still a mother.

"You are blessed, my son!" she cried through her tears. "My heart had withered away—yes, it had died along with you and your father—and now it springs to life just as it did in that first moment when I held you against my chest."

She knelt down and held him close over and over again, while the happiness that couldn't be put into words came out in fragmented sounds, like bubbles rising up to disappear at the surface of a deep spring. The pain of previous years and the darker danger that was approaching didn't cast a shadow on the brightness of that brief moment. Soon, though, the onlookers noticed a change in her expression as awareness of her tragic situation came back, and sorrow filled the well of tears that happiness had opened. From the words she spoke, it seemed that allowing herself to feel natural love had given her mind a brief understanding of her mistakes, and made her realize how far she had wandered from what was right by following the commands of an extreme obsession.

"You've come back to me at such a tragic time, my poor boy," she said, "because your mother's journey has grown darker and darker, and now it ends in death. My son, my son, I carried you in my arms when I could barely stand, and I fed you with food I desperately needed myself; yet I've failed you as a mother throughout your life, and now I'm leaving you nothing but sorrow and disgrace. You'll wander through the world and discover that every heart is shut against you, their kind feelings turned bitter because of me. My child, my child, how much pain lies ahead for your tender soul, and I'm the reason for it all!"

She buried her face against Ilbrahim's head, and her long black hair, dulled with the ashes of grief, cascaded around him like a shroud. A quiet, broken whimper expressed her heart's torment, and it stirred the compassion of many who wrongly believed their natural kindness was sinful. Weeping could be heard from the women's area of the building, and every father present wiped tears from his eyes.

Tobias Pearson felt restless and troubled, weighed down by something that felt like the burden of guilt, preventing him from stepping forward to offer himself as the child's protector. Dorothy, however, had been watching her husband closely. Her mind remained clear of the influence that had started affecting his, and she approached the Quaker woman and spoke to her in front of the entire congregation.

"Stranger, trust this boy to me, and I will be his mother," she said, taking Ilbrahim's hand. "God has clearly chosen my husband to protect him, and he has eaten at our table and stayed under our roof for many days now, until our hearts have grown very attached to him. Leave the gentle child with us, and don't worry about his well-being."

The Quaker stood up from the ground but pulled the boy closer to her while she looked intently into Dorothy's face. Her gentle yet sorrowful features and tidy motherly clothing complemented each other and resembled a verse of comforting poetry. Her very appearance showed that she was innocent, as much as any mortal could be, in her relationship with both God and humanity, while the zealot, dressed in her rough cloth robe and rope belt, had clearly neglected the responsibilities of both this life and the next by focusing entirely on the latter. The two women, each holding one of Ilbrahim's hands, created a living symbol: it was reasonable devotion and uncontrolled extremism fighting for control of a young soul.

"You are not one of our people," said the Quaker, mournfully.

"No, we are not from your community," Dorothy responded gently, "but we are Christians who look toward the same heaven as you do. Don't doubt that your boy will meet you there, if our loving and prayerful guidance of him receives God's blessing. That's where I believe my own children have gone ahead of me, because I too have been a mother. I am no longer one," she continued, her voice trembling, "and your son will receive all my attention."

"But will you guide him down the same path his parents walked?" the Quaker demanded. "Can you teach him the enlightened faith his father died for, and for which I—even I—will soon become an unworthy martyr? The boy has been baptized in blood; will you keep that mark fresh and red on his forehead?"

"I won't lie to you," Dorothy replied. "If your child becomes our child, we have to raise him according to the teachings that Heaven has given us. We have to pray for him using the prayers of our own faith. We have to treat him based on what our own consciences tell us is right, not what yours tells you. If we did anything else, we would be betraying your trust, even while doing what you asked."

The mother gazed down at her son with a worried expression, then lifted her eyes toward the sky. She appeared to be praying silently, and the struggle within her heart was clear to see.

"Friend," she said at last to Dorothy, "I have no doubt that my son will receive all earthly care from you. Indeed, I believe that even your limited understanding may guide him to a better world, for surely you are on that path yourself. But you have spoken of a husband. Is he here among this crowd of people? Let him step forward, for I must know to whom I am entrusting this most precious responsibility."

She turned to face the men in the audience, and after a brief pause, Tobias Pearson stepped forward from the group. The Quaker woman noticed his military uniform and shook her head disapprovingly, but then she observed his uncertain manner, his eyes that tried to meet hers but failed, and the color that flushed and faded across his face as he searched for composure. As she watched him, a joyless smile crossed her face, like sunlight that becomes sad in some abandoned place. Her lips moved silently at first, but finally she spoke:

"I hear it, I hear it! The voice speaks within me and says, 'Leave your child, Catherine, for his place is here, and go away, for I have other work for you. Break the bonds of natural affection, sacrifice your love, and know that in all these things eternal wisdom has its purposes.' I go, friends, I go. Take my boy, my precious jewel. I go away trusting that all shall be well, and that even for his infant hands there is work in the vineyard."

She knelt down and whispered to Ilbrahim, who initially fought against her and held onto his mother while sobbing and crying, but became still after she kissed his cheek and stood up from the ground. After holding her hands above his head in silent prayer, she was prepared to leave.

"Goodbye, friends who helped me in my desperate time," she said to Pearson and his wife; "the kindness you have shown me is a treasure stored in heaven, to be repaid a thousand times over in the future. And goodbye, you who are my enemies, who are not allowed to harm even a single hair on my head, or to stop my journey even for an instant. The day will come when you will ask me to testify on your behalf about this one sin you did not commit, and I will stand up and speak for you."

She walked toward the door, and the men who had positioned themselves as guards stepped aside and allowed her to pass. A widespread feeling of compassion overcame the bitter intensity of religious hatred. Made sacred by her love and her suffering, she departed, and all the people watched her until she had traveled up the hill and disappeared beyond its ridge. She left as the messenger of her own restless heart, to resume the journeys of previous years. Her voice had already been heard throughout many Christian lands, and she had suffered in the cells of a Catholic Inquisition before she experienced the whip and lay imprisoned in Puritan dungeons. Her mission had also reached the followers of the Prophet, and from them she had received the respect and compassion that all the conflicting sects of our supposedly purer faith had joined together to refuse her. She and her husband had lived for many months in Turkey, where even the sultan showed them favor; in that non-Christian land was also Ilbrahim's birthplace, and his Eastern name served as a token of appreciation for the good works of a non-believer.

When Pearson and his wife had gained complete legal guardianship over Ilbrahim, their love for him became as permanent and unchanging as their memories of their homeland or their gentle grief for those who had passed away—it became a fixed part of their hearts. After a week or two of emotional uncertainty, the boy began to show his guardians through countless unconscious actions that he now saw them as his parents and their house as his true home. Before the winter snow had melted away, this persecuted child, this small traveler from a distant and foreign land, appeared to belong naturally in the New England cottage and seemed inseparable from the comfort and safety of its fireplace. Through kind treatment and the knowledge that he was truly loved, Ilbrahim's behavior shed the premature seriousness that had developed from his earlier hardships; he became more like a typical child and his true personality emerged freely. His character was beautiful in many ways, though the troubled minds of both his father and mother had perhaps passed down a certain mental fragility to the boy. In his usual state, Ilbrahim could find joy in the smallest events and in everything around him; he appeared to uncover rich sources of happiness through an ability similar to that of a divining rod, which locates hidden gold where everything appears worthless to the naked eye. His light-hearted cheerfulness, drawn from countless sources, spread to the entire family, and Ilbrahim was like a tamed ray of sunshine, lighting up somber faces and driving away the darkness from the shadowy corners of the cottage.

However, since the capacity for pleasure also means the capacity for pain, the boy's naturally joyful disposition sometimes gave way to periods of deep sadness. The true source of his sorrows couldn't always be traced, but they most often seemed to stem—though Ilbrahim was quite young to be troubled by such things—from hurt feelings. His playful nature often led him to break the strict rules of proper behavior in a Puritan home, and during these times he didn't always avoid being scolded. But the smallest hint of genuine harshness, which he could always tell apart from fake anger, seemed to pierce his heart and ruin all his happiness until he felt completely forgiven again. Ilbrahim completely lacked the spite that usually comes with being overly sensitive. When stepped on, he wouldn't fight back; when hurt, he could only suffer in silence. His mind lacked the strength to stand on its own. He was like a plant that would grow beautifully when wrapped around something stronger than itself, but if pushed away or torn loose, it could only wither and die on the ground. Dorothy's sharp understanding showed her that harsh treatment would break the child's spirit, so she cared for him with the gentle touch of someone handling a delicate butterfly. Her husband showed equal love, though he became less openly affectionate as time went on.

The feelings of the nearby residents toward the Quaker child and those who protected him had not improved, despite the brief moment when the grieving mother had touched their hearts. The contempt and hostility directed at him deeply hurt Ilbrahim, particularly when he realized that children his own age shared their parents' hatred. His gentle and loving nature had already formed strong bonds with everything around him, yet he still had more love to give that he longed to share with the little ones who had been taught to despise him. When the warm spring days arrived, Ilbrahim would spend hours sitting quietly and motionless within earshot of the children playing, but with his characteristic sensitivity, he stayed out of their sight and would run away and hide from even the smallest child among them. Eventually, however, chance seemed to create a way for his heart to connect with theirs through a boy about two years older than Ilbrahim, who got hurt when he fell from a tree near Pearson's home. Since the injured boy's house was quite far away, Dorothy gladly took him in and became his devoted and attentive caregiver.

Ilbrahim possessed an unconscious talent for reading faces, and under different circumstances, this ability would have warned him against trying to befriend this particular boy. The child's face immediately struck observers unpleasantly, though it took careful study to realize that the unsettling effect came from a slight twist of his mouth and the irregular, broken line where his eyebrows nearly met. Perhaps related to these minor deformities was an almost unnoticeable bend in every joint and the uneven bulge of his chest, creating a body that appeared normal in overall shape but flawed in nearly every detail. The boy's personality was moody and withdrawn, and the village schoolmaster labeled him as slow-minded, though later in life he would demonstrate ambition and very unusual abilities. But regardless of his physical or character flaws, Ilbrahim's heart immediately attached itself to him from the moment he was carried wounded into the cottage; the persecuted child seemed to compare his own circumstances with those of this injured boy, feeling that even their different types of suffering had formed a kind of bond between them. Ilbrahim ignored food, rest, and the fresh air he desperately needed; he stayed constantly at the little stranger's bedside and with protective possessiveness tried to be the one through whom all care was given. As the boy began to recover, Ilbrahim created games appropriate for his condition or entertained him using a gift he had perhaps absorbed from the atmosphere of his wild birthplace. This was the ability to tell improvised adventure stories on the spot, apparently in endless variety. His tales were, naturally, fantastical, disconnected, and without clear purpose, but they were fascinating because of a thread of human warmth that ran through all of them, like encountering a dear, familiar face in the middle of strange and otherworldly landscape. The listener paid close attention to these stories and occasionally interrupted with brief comments about the events, showing cleverness beyond his years mixed with a moral corruption that clashed harshly with Ilbrahim's natural goodness. Nothing, however, could stop the growth of Ilbrahim's devotion, and there were many signs that his affection was returned by the dark and stubborn nature he showered it upon. Eventually, the boy's parents took him away to finish his recovery in their own home.

Ilbrahim did not visit his new friend after his departure, but he made worried and constant inquiries about him and found out the day when he would return to play with his companions. On a beautiful summer afternoon, the neighborhood children had gathered in the small forest-surrounded amphitheater behind the meeting-house, and the recovering patient was there, leaning on a walking stick. The joy of twenty pure hearts could be heard in light and cheerful voices that danced among the trees like sunshine made audible; the grown men of this weary world, as they passed by the spot, wondered why life, beginning with such brightness, should continue in darkness, and their hearts or their imaginations answered them, saying that childhood's happiness flows from its innocence. But it happened that an unexpected addition was made to the heavenly little group. It was Ilbrahim, who approached the children with a look of sweet confidence on his beautiful and spiritual face, as if, having shown his love to one of them, he no longer had to fear rejection from their group. A silence fell over their merriment the moment they saw him, and they stood whispering to each other while he came near; but suddenly the devil of their fathers entered into the young fanatics, and, letting out a fierce, sharp cry, they rushed upon the poor Quaker child. In an instant he was surrounded by a group of baby demons, who raised sticks against him, threw stones at him and showed an instinct for destruction far more disgusting than the bloodthirstiness of grown men.

The disabled boy, meanwhile, stood away from the chaos, shouting loudly, "Don't be afraid, Ilbrahim; come over here and take my hand," and his unfortunate friend tried to reach him. After watching the victim's struggling approach with a calm smile and shameless gaze, the cruel little bully raised his stick and hit Ilbrahim in the mouth so hard that blood poured out in a stream. The poor child's arms had been lifted to protect his head from the barrage of strikes, but now he let them fall immediately. His tormentors knocked him down, stomped on him, pulled him by his long blonde hair, and Ilbrahim was about to become as true a martyr as any who ever entered heaven bleeding. The commotion, however, caught the attention of several neighbors, who took the trouble to rescue the little heretic and bring him to Pearson's door.

Ibrahim's physical injuries were severe, but through long and careful nursing, he eventually recovered; however, the damage done to his sensitive soul was more serious, though less visible. The signs were mainly negative in nature and could only be detected by those who had known him before. From that point forward, his walk was slow, steady, and no longer varied by the sudden bursts of lively movement that had once reflected his overflowing joy; his face was heavier, and its former range of expression—like sunlight dancing on moving water—was destroyed by the shadow hanging over his life; he paid far less attention to events happening around him, and he seemed to have much greater difficulty understanding new things than he had during happier times. A stranger basing their opinion on these circumstances would have concluded that the child's mental dullness completely contradicted what his features had promised, but the real explanation lay in where Ibrahim's thoughts were focused—they were turning inward when they should naturally have been exploring the world around him. Dorothy's attempt to bring back his former playfulness was the only time his calm behavior gave way to an intense outburst of sorrow; he broke into passionate crying and ran to hide himself, because his heart had become so painfully tender that even a kind touch felt like fire against it. Sometimes at night, probably in his dreams, he could be heard crying out, "Mother! Mother!" as if her place, which a stranger had filled while Ibrahim was happy, could not be replaced during his terrible suffering. Perhaps among all the weary, miserable people on earth at that time, there was no one who combined innocence and suffering like this poor broken-hearted child, so quickly made a victim of his own pure nature.

While this sorrowful transformation had occurred in Ilbrahim, another change of earlier origin and different nature had reached its completion in his adoptive father. The incident that begins this story found Pearson in a state of spiritual numbness, yet mentally restless and yearning for a more passionate faith than he currently held. The first result of his kindness toward Ilbrahim was to create a gentler feeling, a growing love for the child's entire religious community, but alongside this, and perhaps stemming from self-doubt, was a proud and showy disdain for their beliefs and extreme practices. Through extensive reflection, however—for the topic forced itself persistently into his thoughts—the absurdity of their doctrine began to seem less obvious, and the aspects that had especially troubled his logic took on a different appearance or disappeared completely. The process within him seemed to continue even during sleep, and what had been uncertainty when he went to bed would often become an accepted truth, confirmed by some forgotten reasoning, when he gathered his thoughts in the morning. But while he was gradually becoming similar to these religious zealots, his scorn for them did not diminish at all, instead growing intensely directed at himself; he also believed that every familiar face showed mockery, and that every word spoken to him was a taunt. This was his mental condition during the time of Ilbrahim's tragedy, and the feelings that followed that event completed the transformation for which the child had been the initial catalyst.

Meanwhile, neither the brutality of the persecutors nor the delusion of their victims had lessened. The prison cells were never empty; the streets of nearly every village rang out daily with the sound of whipping; the life of a woman whose gentle and Christian nature no cruelty could make bitter had been taken, and more innocent blood was still to stain the hands that were so frequently lifted in prayer. Shortly after the Restoration, the English Quakers appealed to Charles II that a "vein of blood was open in his dominions," but although the indulgent king's anger was stirred, his intervention was not swift. And now the story must leap forward across many months, leaving Pearson to face shame and hardship; his wife, to steadfast endurance of countless griefs; poor Ilbrahim, to waste away and wither like a diseased rose-bud; his mother, to wander on a misguided mission, neglecting the most sacred duty that can be entrusted to a woman.

A winter evening filled with stormy weather had settled over Pearson's home, and there were no happy faces present to chase away the darkness from his wide fireplace. The fire did indeed give off warm heat and a reddish glow, and large logs dripping with partially melted snow lay ready to be thrown onto the burning coals. However, the room looked sad due to the absence of much of the simple household wealth that had once decorated it, because the demands of repeated fines and his own neglect of worldly matters had severely impoverished the owner. Along with the furnishings of peace, the tools of war had also vanished; the sword was broken, the helmet and armor were thrown away forever: the soldier was finished with battles, and could not even raise his bare hand to protect his head. But the Holy Book remained, and the table it rested on was pulled close to the fire, while two members of the persecuted sect looked for comfort in its pages.

The man who listened while the other read was the master of the house, now thin and gaunt with a changed expression and unhealthy complexion, because his mind had spent too much time lost in imaginary thoughts and his body had been weakened by imprisonment and beatings. The robust and weather-worn old man sitting next to him had suffered less damage from a much longer period of living the same way. He was tall and dignified in appearance, and his gray hair fell from beneath his wide-brimmed hat and rested on his shoulders—something that alone would have made the Puritans despise him. As the old man read from the holy book, snow drifted against the windows and swirled in through the cracks around the door, while wind laughed in the chimney and flames leaped wildly upward to meet it. Sometimes, when the wind hit the hill at just the right angle and swept down past the cottage across the frozen plain, its sound was the most mournful imaginable; it seemed as though the past itself was speaking, as if each of the dead had added their whisper, as if the loneliness of countless ages was carried in that single sorrowful cry.

The Quaker finally closed the book, though he kept his hand between the pages he had been reading, while he stared intently at Pearson. Pearson's posture and expression might have suggested he was enduring physical pain; he rested his forehead in his hands, his teeth were clenched tight, and his body shook periodically with nervous tension.

"Friend Tobias," asked the old man with compassion, "have you found no comfort in these many blessed passages of Scripture?"

"Your voice has reached my ear like a distant and unclear sound," Pearson replied, without raising his eyes. "Yes; and when I have listened carefully, the words seemed cold and lifeless and meant for someone else and a smaller grief than mine. Take the book away," he added, in a tone of sullen bitterness; "I have no place in its comfort, and it only makes my sorrow worse."

"No, weak brother; don't be like someone who has never known the light," said the older Quaker, seriously, but with gentleness. "Are you the one who would be willing to give everything and endure everything for the sake of conscience, even wanting special trials so that your faith might be made pure and your heart turned away from worldly desires? And will you collapse under a suffering that happens equally to those who have their reward here on earth and to those who store up treasure in heaven? Don't lose heart, for your burden is still light."

"It's too much! It's more than I can handle!" Pearson cried out, his changeable nature showing through his impatience. "Since I was young, I've been marked for suffering, and year after year—yes, day after day—I've endured pain that others never experience in their entire lives. And I'm not even talking about the love that turned into hate, the honor that became shame, or how comfort and abundance became danger, poverty, and having nothing. I could have endured all of that and still considered myself fortunate. But when my heart was empty from so many losses, I gave my love to a stranger's child, and he became more precious to me than all those I've buried; and now he must die too, as if my love were poison. Truly, I am a cursed man, and I will lie down in the dirt and never raise my head again."

"You sin, brother, but it's not my place to criticize you, because I too have experienced dark times when I complained against suffering," said the old Quaker. He went on, perhaps hoping to take his companion's mind off his own troubles: "Even recently the light was dimmed within me, when the violent men had exiled me under threat of death and the officers escorted me from village to village toward the wilderness. A strong and merciless hand was handling the knotted ropes; they cut deep into the skin, and you could have followed every stumble and stagger of my steps by the blood that trailed behind. As we continued—"

"Haven't I endured all of this without complaining?" Pearson interrupted impatiently.

"No, friend, but listen to me," the other man went on. "As we traveled forward, night fell across our path, making it impossible for anyone to see the fury of those who hunted us or how steadfast I remained in my suffering, though God forbid I should take pride in such endurance. Lights started to flicker in the cottage windows, and I could make out the people inside as they gathered in warmth and safety, each man with his wife and children around their own evening fireplace. Eventually we reached an area of rich, fertile ground. In the fading light, the forest surrounding it wasn't visible, and there before us stood a straw-roofed house that looked exactly like my home far across the vast ocean—far away in our own England. Then painful thoughts flooded over me—yes, memories that felt like death to my very soul. The joy of my younger days appeared before me, the restlessness of my adult years, the changed beliefs of my later life. I recalled how I had felt compelled to leave and become a wanderer when my daughter, the youngest and most beloved of my children, lay dying in her bed, and—"

"Could you obey the command at such a moment?" exclaimed Pearson, shuddering.

"Yes! Yes!" the old man replied hastily. "I was kneeling beside her bed when the voice spoke loudly within me, but I immediately stood up, took my staff, and left. Oh, if only I could forget the sorrowful look on her face when I pulled away my arm and left her to journey through the dark valley alone! Her soul was weak and she had depended on my prayers. During that horrible night, I was tormented by the thought that I had been a misguided Christian and a heartless father; yes, even my daughter with her pale, dying face seemed to stand beside me and whisper, 'Father, you are wrong; go home and find shelter for your gray head.'— O You whom I have looked to in my farthest travels," the Quaker continued, lifting his troubled eyes to heaven, "do not inflict upon even the most violent of our persecutors the complete agony of my soul when I believed that everything I had done and suffered for you was at the urging of a mocking devil!—But I did not give in; I knelt down and struggled with the tempter, while the whip cut more savagely into my flesh. My prayer was answered, and I continued on in peace and joy toward the wilderness."

The elderly man, though his passionate beliefs usually carried all the composure of logical thought, was profoundly stirred as he told this story, and his unusual display of feeling appeared to silence and suppress his companion's emotions. They remained quiet, their faces turned toward the fire, perhaps envisioning in its glowing coals fresh scenes of suffering they might yet face. The snow continued to blow forcefully against the windows, and occasionally, as the flame from the logs had slowly diminished, it drifted down the large chimney and sizzled on the hearth. A careful footstep could sometimes be detected in an adjacent room, and the noise consistently caused both Quakers to look toward the door that opened in that direction. When a violent and turbulent burst of wind had brought his mind through natural connection to wandering travelers on such an evening, Pearson continued their discussion.

"I have nearly collapsed under my own burden of this ordeal," he said, letting out a heavy sigh; "yet I wish it could be doubled for me, if only the child's mother could be spared. Her wounds have been deep and numerous, but this will be the most painful of all."

"Don't worry about Catharine," the old Quaker responded, "because I know that brave woman and have witnessed how she can endure hardship. A mother's love runs deep within her and might appear to struggle greatly against her faith, but soon she will rise and express gratitude that her son became an accepted offering so young. The boy has completed his purpose, and she will understand that he was taken away as an act of mercy for both him and her. Blessed, truly blessed are those who can find peace with so little pain!"

The restless gusting of the wind was suddenly interrupted by an ominous sound: rapid, heavy pounding at the front door. Pearson's already pale face turned even whiter, as countless experiences with persecution had taught him what to fear; the elderly man, however, straightened up tall, and his gaze was as steady as that of a battle-tested soldier waiting for his enemy.

"The violent men have come looking for me," he said calmly. "They've learned that I was compelled to return from exile, and now I'm going to be taken to prison, and from there to my death. This is an ending I've been expecting for a long time. I will open the door to them so they cannot say, 'Look, he's afraid!'"

"No; I will go before them myself," said Pearson, his courage returning. "It may be that they're looking for me alone and don't know that you're staying with me."

"Let's go boldly, both of us," his companion replied. "It wouldn't be right for either you or me to back down."

They walked through the entryway to the door, which they opened, telling the visitor "Come in, in God's name!" A fierce gust of wind blew the storm directly into their faces and put out the lamp; they could just barely make out a figure so completely white from head to toe with blown snow that it looked like Winter itself had taken human form to seek shelter from its own bleakness.

"Come in, friend, and tell me what you need, whatever it might be," said Pearson. "It must be urgent, since you're out on such a harsh night."

"Peace be with this household!" said the stranger, when they stood on the floor of the inner room.

Pearson jumped; the older Quaker stirred the sleeping coals of the fire until they created a bright and towering flame. A woman's voice had spoken; a woman's figure appeared, cold and stark, in that warm light.

"Catherine, blessed woman," the old man exclaimed, "have you returned to this darkened land once more? Have you come to bear courageous witness as you did in years past? The persecution has not defeated you, and you have emerged victorious from the prison, but strengthen your heart now, Catherine, for Heaven will test you one final time before you receive your reward."

"Rejoice, friends!" she replied. "You who have long been part of our community, and you whom a little child has brought to us, rejoice! Look, I come as the messenger of good news, for the time of persecution has ended. The heart of the king, Charles himself, has been moved with compassion toward us, and he has sent out his orders to stop the violent men. A ship full of our friends has arrived at that town over there, and I sailed joyfully with them."

As Catherine spoke, her eyes wandered around the room, searching for the person who made safety so precious to her. Pearson silently pleaded with the old man, and the elderly gentleman didn't shy away from the difficult responsibility placed upon him.

"Sister," he began, speaking in a gentle yet completely calm voice, "you tell us about his love shown through earthly blessings, and now we must speak to you about that same love displayed through trials and hardships. Until now, Catherine, you have been like someone traveling on a dark and difficult path while leading a small child by the hand; you would have wanted to look toward heaven constantly, but the needs of that little child kept drawing your eyes and your heart back to earthly concerns. Sister, continue to rejoice, for his unsteady steps will no longer slow down your own progress."

The grieving mother could not be comforted so easily. She trembled uncontrollably; her face became as pale as the snow that had blown into her hair. The resolute old man reached out his hand to steady her, maintaining eye contact as though to prevent any emotional outburst.

"I am a woman—I am only a woman; will He test me beyond what I can bear?" said Catherine, speaking very quickly and almost in a whisper. "I have been deeply wounded; I have endured so much—many physical sufferings, many mental anguishes; tormented within myself and through those who were most precious to me. Surely," she added, with a long shudder, "he has spared me in this one matter." She burst out with sudden and uncontrollable fury: "Tell me, man with a cold heart, what has God done to me? Has he struck me down never to rise again? Has he crushed my very heart in his hand?—And you to whom I entrusted my child, how have you honored that trust? Give me back the boy healthy, unharmed, alive—alive—or earth and heaven will seek revenge for me!"

The anguished scream of Catharine was answered by the weak—the extremely weak—voice of a child.

On this day it had become clear to Pearson, to his elderly guest, and to Dorothy that Ilbrahim's short and troubled journey was nearing its end. The two men would have gladly stayed by his side to offer the prayers and religious words they believed were fitting for this moment, and which, even if they cannot help the departing soul's welcome in the world where he is going, might at least comfort him as he says goodbye to earth. But although Ilbrahim made no complaint, he was unsettled by the faces watching him, so Dorothy's pleas and their own belief that the child's feet might walk on heaven's floor without staining it had convinced the two Quakers to leave. Ilbrahim then closed his eyes and became peaceful, and except for an occasional kind and quiet word to his caretaker, he might have seemed to be sleeping. As evening approached, however, and the storm began to build, something appeared to disturb the boy's peace of mind and make his hearing sharp and sensitive. If a passing breeze lingered to rattle the window, he tried to turn his head toward it; if the door creaked back and forth on its hinges, he looked long and worriedly in that direction; if the deep voice of the old man as he read the Scriptures rose even slightly higher, the child almost held his failing breath to listen; if a pile of snow swept past the cottage with a sound like fabric dragging,

Ilbrahim seemed to watch for some visitor to enter. But after a short while he gave up whatever secret hope had stirred him and with one quiet, sorrowful whisper turned his cheek against the pillow. He then spoke to Dorothy with his usual gentleness and asked her to come closer to him; she did so, and Ilbrahim took her hand in both of his, holding it with a soft grip, as if to make sure he still had hold of it. At times, and without disturbing the calm of his expression, a very slight trembling passed through him from head to foot, as if a gentle but somewhat cold breeze had touched him and made him shiver.

As the boy guided her by the hand through his peaceful journey toward the boundaries of eternity, Dorothy almost felt she could make out the nearby yet faint beauty of the home he was approaching; she wouldn't have tempted the small traveler to turn back, even though she grieved that she would have to leave him behind and return to this world. But just as Ilbrahim's feet were stepping onto the ground of Paradise, he heard a voice calling from behind him, and it drew him back a few short steps along the difficult path he had already walked. When Dorothy looked at his face, she noticed that the calm expression had become troubled once more. Her thoughts had been so completely focused on him that she hadn't heard the sounds of the storm or any human voices around her; but when Catharine's scream cut through the room, the boy struggled to lift himself up.

"Friend, she has arrived! Open the door for her!" he shouted.

In an instant, his mother was kneeling beside the bed; she pulled Ilbrahim close to her chest, and he settled there without any overwhelming burst of happiness, but peacefully as though he were calming himself to fall asleep.

He gazed up at her face, and seeing her anguish, spoke with weak but sincere intensity,

"Don't cry, dearest mother. I am happy now;" and with these words the gentle boy died.

The king's order to stop the New England persecutors was effective in preventing further executions, but the colonial authorities, relying on the distance of their location, and perhaps on the perceived instability of the royal government, soon resumed their harsh treatment in all other ways. Catharine's religious extremism had grown more intense through the breaking of all human connections; and wherever a whip was raised, there she was to receive the strike; and whenever a prison cell was opened, there she went to throw herself upon the ground. But over time a more Christian attitude—a spirit of tolerance, though not of warmth or approval—began to spread throughout the land regarding the persecuted religious group. And then, when the stern old Pilgrims looked at her with pity rather than anger, when the women fed her with scraps from their children's meals and offered her a place to sleep on a hard and humble bed, when no small group of schoolboys abandoned their games to throw stones at the wandering zealot,—then Catharine returned to Pearson's house, and made that her home.

As if Ibrahim's gentle nature still surrounded his remains, as if his kind spirit descended from heaven to show his mother the path to true faith, her harsh and vengeful character was mellowed by the same sorrows that had once made it worse. When years had passed and the quiet mourner's face became a familiar sight in the community, she became someone who drew not profound but widespread concern—a person upon whom everyone's extra compassion could be freely given. Everyone spoke of her with the kind of sympathy that feels good to offer; everyone was willing to show her small acts of kindness that cost little but demonstrate goodwill; and when she finally passed away, a long procession of those who had once been her bitter enemies followed her with respectful grief and tears that brought no pain to her resting place beside Ibrahim's overgrown and settled grave.

THE END

Thank You For Reading

You've Just Read a Piece of the Greatest Library Ever Rebuilt

Thank you for reading.

This book is one of thousands we're restoring, reimagining, and translating as part of the **Modern Library of Alexandria** — a global movement to preserve and share humanity's most important ideas.

What was once lost to fire and time is now rising again — not just as memory, but as living, breathing knowledge, freely accessible to all.

What You Can Do Next:

- **Keep Reading.**

  Discover more legendary works — in beautiful print, audiobook, or digital form — at LibraryofAlexandria.com.

- **Build Your Own Library.**

  Every title is available as a paperback, hardcover, or collectible boxset — at true printing cost. Craft a personal library worthy of display.

- **Spread the Light.**

  Share this book. Tell others about the movement. Help us translate every timeless work into every language, so no reader is ever left behind.

By finishing this book, you've already taken part in something extraordinary.

Join us at LibraryofAlexandria.com

Together, we're rebuilding the greatest library the world has ever known.

With appreciation,

The Modern Library of Alexandria Team

Visit:
www.libraryofalexandria.com
Or scan the code below: